MISSING

IN THE

MINARETS

MISSING

IN THE

MINARETS

THE SEARCH
for
WALTER A. STARR,
JR.

WILLIAM
ALSUP

YOSEMITE CONSERVANCY
YOSEMITE NATIONAL PARK

YOSEMITE
CONSERVANCY.

yosemiteconservancy.org

Yosemite Conservancy inspires people to support projects and
programs that preserve Yosemite and enrich the visitor experience.

Pages 2–3:
Clyde Minaret from Minaret Lake.
Photograph by Stephen H. Willard,
from the collection of Walter A. Starr, Sr.

ISBN 978-1-930238-18-3

For Suzan, Allison, and John—
and every camp they brightened.

Contents

Foreword

There have been two searches for Walter A. Starr, Jr., one in 1933 described in this book, and the other the search by the author, William Alsup, a recent one for the evidence presented in this book. Bill has been relentless in his search, taking the blurred memories, faded photographs, and crumbling summit records to reconstruct the original events. With a trial lawyer's skill and persistence, he has crafted a readable and authentic contribution to Sierra literature. It involves not only the search, but also the geography and history of the Minarets and the California High Sierra.

It was my privilege to have some part in both searches, sixty-six years apart, but Bill now knows more about what I did on the Minarets in August 1933 than I now remember. There have been many changes in those sixty-odd years. In 1933, the Sierra Club still conducted well-organized expeditions with pack animals and kitchens called High Trips. There was still a seemingly endless supply of firewood, no permits, no reservations or regulations, and meeting another party was a rarity. In 1933, Francis Farquhar usually saved my letters to answer in person, or if urgent, communicated with me by Western Union. Now, information can be transmitted with the speed of electronic mail.

I learned to rock climb with Ernest Dawson, Norman Clyde, William Horsfall, Jules Eichorn, Richard Jones, Ansel Adams, Robert Underhill, and many others. Every day was a new day of exploration and discovery of the unspoiled beauty of meadows, cascading streams, lakes, flowers, trees, and rocks. We enjoyed finding summit records of other climbers, and even discovered previously unclimbed peaks. My climbing career spanned from the time before the use of ropes to the beginnings of technical rock climbing. We were not concerned with insurance or liability. We knew there were risks involved but felt they were *our* risks.

In September of 1992, Jules Eichorn and I took a short walk together along the base of Lembert Dome in Tuolumne Meadows, not to climb, but to admire the glacial polish, the cliffs and trees, and to remember. Part of those memories are in this book. Much may have happened since 1933, but the High Sierra still remains a wondrous Range of Light.

Glen Dawson
Pasadena, California

Introduction

Here among the rare manuscripts in the reading room of the Bancroft Library at the University of California at Berkeley, I pull a small, letter-sized envelope from an archive folder. The handwriting on it reads, "To Mr. Starr from Jules Eichorn." The envelope, faded with age, was opened on one end long ago. Carefully, I remove a thin rectangle of cardboard with soft ragged edges, the envelope's only contents. "Kodak Film" is printed on the yellow side. On the unfinished reverse are penciled signatures under the date August 3, 1931. The first name written is that of Norman Clyde, and it is followed by three others. Rotating the card, I see another name and date along the card's left edge running perpendicular to those names. The notation is printed by hand; no, it is *painted* by hand, in rust red. It reads "W. A. Starr" with "Aug 6 32" beneath the name.

I pause to reflect. The library walls are partitioned by tall windows, their shutters drawn open. Autumn storm light illuminates the chamber. Historic paintings of California grace the room. Thomas Hill's "Yosemite Valley from Inspiration Point" brightens the wall beside me. At eight long tables, students and scholars are scattered about, reverently bent over musty archives. Librarians stand guard at their massive bunker in the center. Pencils only!—no residue of history will be marred with ink here.

I realize that finding this artifact is an amazing stroke of luck. I should have come across it in a different file and carton at the Bancroft, but my searching did not uncover it. On a hunch, I had decided to test whether it had been misfiled. With an educated guess, I had asked for the folder on Mountain Registers marked "Clyde Minaret 1948–." And in that folder, in fact, it was and is. I stare at the cardboard record again, re-read the first names, rotate the fragment, then re-read Starr's entry. It is faded red. It dawns on me that Starr really did sketch his name and the date in blood, more meticulously than I would have thought possible in the circumstances. Here on a single scrap, once left atop a mountain peak and now misplaced among inert archives, are the signatures of two legendary Sierra mountaineers. There is, I think, a tale here, a story about these names, about this record and the place it was made—a magnificent moment in mountaineering that deserves to be told with as much accuracy as can be divined after the passage of seventy years.

William Alsup
Oakland, California

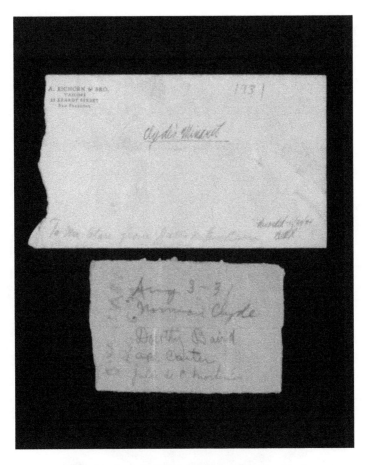

When Pete Starr climbed Clyde Minaret in 1932 he arrived
without a pencil and cut his ear for blood to scratch his name
for the record. Today the record is in
the Bancroft Museum at Berkeley.

*Peter Starr in the Ritter Range. This photograph was taken
of Peter Starr on a group outing via Agnew Pass to climb
Mt. Ritter on July 4, 1932. The photograph was taken by
fellow climber Harley Stevens and is from
the collection of Walter A. Starr, Sr.*

CHAPTER I

Walter ("Peter") A. Starr, Jr.

On July 29, 1933, a Saturday, Walter A. Starr, Jr., left the San Francisco area for two weeks of solo exploration in the Sierra Nevada. He was thirty, single, athletic, handsome, a lawyer as it happened, but most of all a mountaineer. Starr was in the fourth year of an audacious, one-person project to survey the recently completed John Muir Trail (a route running over 211 miles from Yosemite Valley to the summit of Mt. Whitney) and the surrounding High Sierra. He planned to prepare a guidebook for the mighty range including route information for mountaineering ascents of its major peaks.[1]

Starr had scaled forty or more prominent mountains in the Sierra and had kept notes of his experiences. He had hiked practically all of the John Muir Trail and its lateral spurs, making scribbles on mileage, elevation gains, notable vistas, available forage, and places to camp. His summer vacations had been lavished on such expeditions. So too had many a weekend during which he had driven through nights on both ends to maximize his mountain time. A college track star, he had phenomenal endurance and the ability to hike swiftly over many miles, hours on end, by daylight, moonlight, even starlight. Once, on a four-and-a-half-day reconnaissance in the Sierra, he covered 143 miles. He usually hiked and climbed alone. He always climbed without a rope.[2]

He went by the nickname Peter. A graduate of Oakland Technical High School, he entered Stanford University in 1921, and there earned both college and law degrees in only five years, while compiling an outstanding academic record. He was outgoing, vivacious, and sociable. Like his father, he joined the fraternity Delta Kappa Epsilon.

Upon finishing law school, Peter took nine months abroad in Europe and Africa in 1926 and 1927, financed by his father and mother, who were both from old California families. His letters home embraced high adventure, dining at the Ritz, veiled suggestions of romance, fun with fraternity brothers, descriptions of art museums, ancient cathedrals, leaning towers, and grand hotels, and allusions to future war.[3] With two guides, he reached the pinnacle of Mont Blanc. Peter described the final push in a letter to his father:

> Upon arriving at the refuge, I had one of the shocks of my life. I had always imagined the summit of Mont Blanc to be a nicely rounded dome, in fact it appears as such from Chamonix. But it was evident upon arriving at the refuge that what appeared to be flat from below was a steep sawtooth ridge with "hardly room to stand on" it. Being at such a height the snow was well frozen (almost ice) so that however hard you struck your feet into it you could barely make any impression and even the ice picks [ice axes] were unable to make much impression. As it would take too long, steps were cut only in the worst places and then most insecure. Due to the sharpness of the arete, the top was absolutely not the least bit flat but came to a pointed ridge along which one walked pigeon toed with one foot on one side, the other on the other. Thousands of feet dropped on either side as approximate to perpendicularity as possible below to glaciers below on either side—solid ice so no feeling of security. If anyone slid, I don't see how the others could hold on as the ice picks made practically no entry into the surface.[4]

Starr returned to California, passed the bar examination, and commenced law practice in 1927 at 225 Bush Street in San Francisco, on the sixteenth floor of the Standard Oil Building, with the law firm of Pillsbury, Madison & Sutro, then as today a leading institution in California. The firm had twenty lawyers, a huge number for a California law firm in those days. The University Club

in San Francisco admitted Peter. His
secretary remembered that "Mr. Starr"
(lawyers were known by their last names
in those days) rarely shined his shoes
and would stretch out on the floor in the
firm's library and read.[5]

In a photograph of Peter Starr taken
in July 1932 near Mt. Ritter in the Sierra,
the rock and snow at timberline (a peak
looming in the distance) furnished a set-
ting where one could more easily imagine
scuffed footwear and horizontal reading. Relaxing, he sat on a boulder, legs
crossed, wearing knickers, undershirt,
knee-high socks, and basketball shoes, the
conventional rock-climbing footwear of
the era. He was young, tall, trim, tanned,
even debonair, and brimming with con-
fidence. He had long limbs and dark hair,
and his engaging smile teased the camera
(see page 14).[6]

Peter Starr (right) on top of Mt.
Clarence King, 1929.
Photograph by Allan Starr.

While in law school and in the early years of law practice, he hiked on
occasion with his brother, Allan, who was four years his junior. Their last
trip in 1929, shared with a mutual pal, was one to envy. They all met in Independence, California, a historic desert crossroads in the dry Owens Valley.
Through the pale colors of the eastern slope of the Sierra, they drove up to
Onion Valley, the trail head for Kearsarge Pass. There they rented a mule and
a donkey to carry their gear and headed off into the most scenic and dramatic
region of the southern Sierra, a pantheon of peaks that would later become
Kings Canyon National Park. At Kearsarge Pass, thousands of feet higher,
they crested the divide between wet and dry. The vista back captured the

Peter Starr wrote on the reverse side of this print:
"Middle Palisade and glacier from Mt. Sill."
Photograph by Peter Starr.

faded hues of the land of little rain; the view ahead shone in brilliant shades of green and blue, white and gray.

The three men dropped quickly down to Bullfrog Lake and then farther still to Vidette Meadow, where they camped in the shade along the cascades of Bubbs Creek. Via East Lake, an exquisite jewel set beneath the Kings-Kern Divide, they climbed Mt. Brewer (13,577 feet), first ascended in 1864 by Professor William Brewer, who led the field party of the California Geological Survey. The survey had believed that Brewer was the highest peak in the Sierra, only to find, once on top, that a yet-taller group clustered around a summit they soon called Mt. Whitney, after their survey chief.

Lake Reflection.
Photograph by Peter Starr.

Inconsolables and Palisades from Dusy Basin.
Photograph by Peter Starr.

Turning north, the Starr party marched up the John Muir Trail to Glen Pass, then down to Rae Lakes, laying over to explore Sixty Lakes Basin. Next, they made the summit of Mt. Clarence King (12,909 feet), named for another member of the 1864 survey expedition (see page 17).[7] Forging into Paradise Valley, they continued over Cartridge Pass to Marion Lake, and thence to the Palisades Region, one of two groups of Sierra peaks over 14,000 feet (the other being the Whitney group further south). Allan and Ralph climbed the North Palisade while Peter, having already done "North Pal," climbed Mt. Sill and Polemonium Peak (see page 18).[8] Most of the trip was at timberline or above, affording unobstructed panoramas of crag upon crag, ridge above gorge, some of the grandest high mountain scenery in the United States. They left over Bishop Pass after covering more than one hundred miles. "The end of a perfect trip," wrote Allan in his photo scrap book.[9]

Thereafter, the brothers took different paths. Allan became consumed by automotive mechanics, married, and by July 1933 when Peter left for the mountains, was a new father. A bachelor, Peter devoted himself to his guide-book project. Although he enjoyed company on the trail, he increasingly

Wanda Lake photographed by Peter Starr.

[20]

found himself alone and relishing his intimacy with talus and timber. In this, Starr was a paradox. On the one hand, he was outgoing, the sociable son of a prominent family, a joiner in college and career. On the other, at least in the wild, he preferred the companionship of the landscape itself. Bark to core, he was an unrepentant romantic about the granite heights. Accounts of mountain adventures in the *Sierra Club Bulletin* brightened his sleep.

The early mountain registers of the Sierra are replete with Starr's prose. A typical example is his entry dated August 22, 1930, on Middle Palisade:

Peter Starr with a heavy pack, canteen, and Kodak case with friends on way to climb Mt. Shasta, May 1931. From the collection of Walter A. Starr, Sr.

W. A. Starr, Jr.   Sierra Club   With exception of Langley this completes ascent of all Sierran 14,000 ft. peaks. Last year I ascended Peak Disappointment (southernmost point of ridge with large cairn) from northeastern side. Proceeded along ridge, dropped down almost to glacier and ascended chute to crest just south of peak, a very thrilling climb and feasible from Owens Valley side by proceeding to low point on crest beyond southern end of glacier.[10]

By 1933, Starr had already written most of his guide, even its introduction. "It is to be hoped," he said, "that this marvelous region traversed by the Muir Trail will never be opened up by motor roads, but will be kept inviolate, reserved as a wilderness area." The highest of the high country was his venue of choice: "I am an ardent lover of the mountains and admire all mountain scenery; but while the type of country in the lower and middle Sierra pleases me, the High Sierra fascinates and thrills me. . . In the vacation months, when it is hot, dry, and dusty, in the middle and lower Sierra, it is springtime in my strip of blue lakes through which winds the Muir Trail."[11]

In addition to his prose, music and verse were Peter's artistic outlets. Starting at an early age, in fact, he had written much poetry and often played the piano. Only a few days before leaving for the Sierra in 1933, he penned a verse entitled "The Mountain's Call." Its last line read: "Defiant mountains beckon me to glory and dream in their paradise."[12]

Now, on a Saturday at the end of July 1933, springtime had arrived in the High Sierra. Columbines, gentians, paintbrushes, shooting stars, primroses—sky pilots at the passes—all these and a hundred more wildflowers blazed along the crest. After a very mild winter, the entire range was wide open. Starr was off again with his ice-axe, crampons, note pad, Kodak, and other camp gear. Later, when it would matter, no one would know exactly where he had headed. It was only known that he had intended to drive to the east side of the Sierra, the magnificent side where the slope rises abruptly, a journey through the Yosemite backcountry over the Tioga Pass Road, a six-hour trip today, even longer then. The only announced plan was to meet his father eventually at a rustic trailhead resort on the east side called Glacier Lodge. The rendez-vous was set for August 7.[13]

Tuolumne Meadows and the
Tioga Pass Road as it looked in 1932.
Photograph by Peter Starr.

Peter Starr and Whiting Welch on July 27, 1933.
From the collection of Walter A. Starr, Sr.

CHAPTER 2

Missing

On August 7, Walter A. Starr, Sr., waited for his son at Glacier Lodge. Situated at 7,800 feet on the east side of the Sierra, between the Owens Valley and the crest, the lodge stood at the traditional trailhead for the Palisades region, with its cluster of peaks over 14,000 feet. A watering hole for the Sierra cognoscenti, Glacier Lodge consisted of a few cabins and a crude main hall, rendered spectacular in the reflected glory of the Palisades.[14]

The elder Mr. Starr, then 56, was a magnetic combination of adventurer and entrepreneur, who had attracted an influential and successful set of friends. He was decisive yet courteous. And he was fit, being quite a mountaineer himself. After graduating from the University of California at Berkeley in the summer of 1896 at age nineteen, he and a fraternity brother, Allen Chickering (who later built a respected law firm in San Francisco), embarked on a mountaineering first.

Both had joined the Sierra Club in 1894.[15] Through the club, they became acquainted with Theodore Solomons, the famed mountaineer obsessed with finding a high-country route from Yosemite to Kings Canyon, and whose determination inspired the John Muir Trail itself. Solomons had made three previous Sierran explorations and agreed to undertake a fourth with Chickering and Starr.[16] On July 3, 1896, the trio left Yosemite Valley with four horses, headed southeast. About two weeks later, however, Solomons took ill and had to drop out.

Starr and Chickering pushed on, veering west into mountain elevations a few thousand feet below the crest. Because the United States Geological

*On their 1896 trip from Yosemite to Kings Canyon, Starr and Chickering made this
image inscribed by Mr. Starr as "Mt. Ritter and the Minarets." Michael Minaret
appears as the tallest spire. This view is from the west looking east.
From the collection of Walter A. Starr, Sr.*

Walter A. Starr, Sr., in the Yukon about 1899, from his collection.

Survey had not yet mapped the region, one of the young men's objectives was to obtain topographic data and photographs to assist Professor Joseph Le Conte, Jr., in making his Sierra Club maps of the High Sierra.[17] For vistas of the terrain, they climbed peaks. On July 21, they made the top of the dark and brooding ruin of Mt. Goddard.[18] They were the first of record to ascend Tehipite Dome.[19] Finally, they triumphantly marched into Kings Canyon on August 3. Although they did not achieve a true high route, they remained high enough to be credited with the first trek directly through the Sierra from Yosemite to Kings Canyon (with pack animals).[20]

The next year, at age twenty, Mr. Starr "crammed two semesters into one in order to get enough credits to graduate," and then joined in the rush for gold in the Klondike.[21] (Coincidentally, so did Solomons, and they ran into each other at Lake Bennett.) The excursion proved high on adventure but low on gold.[22] Mr. Starr then took work packing mail in the Yukon. He eventually returned to the Bay Area via Seattle. He went into the grain and export business, starting from scratch because his family wealth had been consumed in the Panic of 1893.

In 1902, Walter Starr married Carmen Moore, also a Cal grad, whose grandparents had crossed the plains in covered wagons, and whose father was a prominent attorney in Oakland. Carmen and Walter had two children—Peter, born in 1903, and Allan, born in 1907. In 1911, the Starrs engaged the well-known architect Julia Morgan to design a graceful home on Hampton Road in Piedmont in the East Bay hills.[23]

Carmen Starr, Peter's mother.

Carmen's father owned a large tract of land, a hobby ranch northeast of San Jose high on the ridges near Mission Peak. There, young Peter and Allan built elaborate tree houses among the oaks during their summer recesses. Peter regularly slept in his tree house through the summer months. There, too, he wrote poetry, inspired by Mission Peak. In 1915, at the age of twelve, Peter compiled a booklet of poems entitled *Verses From the Hill Top Tree*. Carmen cherished it.[24]

In 1927, the Starrs re-engaged architect Morgan to design another home, this time a summer ranch home (and guest cottage) on a forty-acre corner carved out of the Mission Peak Ranch owned by Carmen's parents. The Starrs added a pool and a tennis court, as they developed an altogether comfortable private retreat. The Starr family then spent a large part of the warmer months at the ranch, entertaining the descendants of Old California, including professors, intellectuals, ranchers, and even President Herbert Hoover.

While attending college and law school, and later as he worked his way into law practice, Peter often spent weekends at the ranch with various combinations of fraternity brothers and family friends. Starr family fun and milestones were recorded by Carmen in a diary she called the "ranch book." Her last entry for July 1933 described Peter's day of tennis and swimming enjoyed with fraternity brother Whiting Welch, a day before Welch's wedding. On July 29, she wrote that Peter left immediately after the wedding "on his vacation to his beloved mountains."[25]

❋   ❋   ❋

August 7 passed. Peter did not arrive at Glacier Lodge. The next day, he still
did not appear. On August 9, Walter Starr left to return home, anxious and
concerned. He felt that his son must have changed his plans and decided, for
some reason, not to come out of the mountains at Glacier Lodge. The word of
Peter's no-show spread locally. The renowned mountaineer, Norman Clyde,
had been exploring the Palisade Glacier when he heard the news, having just
returned from the Sierra Club's annual "High Trip." Clyde later wrote that he
thought "something unusual" must have occurred, for it was out of character
for someone such as Peter Starr to miss an appointment.[26]

One might wonder why the elder Mr. Starr did not initiate a search before
heading home. Then, as now, the vast majority of overdue hikers walk out
on their own within a day or so. It is usually not worth putting others at risk
too soon, especially when the missing party is a skilled mountaineer. In Starr's
case, the benign possibilities were multiple. Starr tentatively planned to come
down to Glacier Lodge from the Sierra, to re-provision there and continue
south along the John Muir Trail. He was not due to return home until August
13.[27] Given his ongoing project to develop a guidebook to the mountains, any
number of plausible obstacles might have detained him, such as a side trip
to explore a lateral trail. And if anyone could take care of himself among the
granite clefts, it was Peter—of that Mr. Starr was certain.

When Peter Starr did not arrive for work on August 14, however, his
father immediately asked the authorities for help. As they organized, officials
were uncertain about where to start. The first step was to determine the location of the missing hiker's car. Late on the fourteenth, patrols began to comb
the east side and its many trailheads, checking the ends of the dirt roads that
zigzagged up through interleaved canyons of the Mammoth Lakes country,
the Glacier Lodge area, Onion Valley, and the Lone Pine Canyons.

By that evening, the story had captured the attention of newspapers in
the San Francisco Bay Area, Los Angeles, the Central Valley, and the Owens

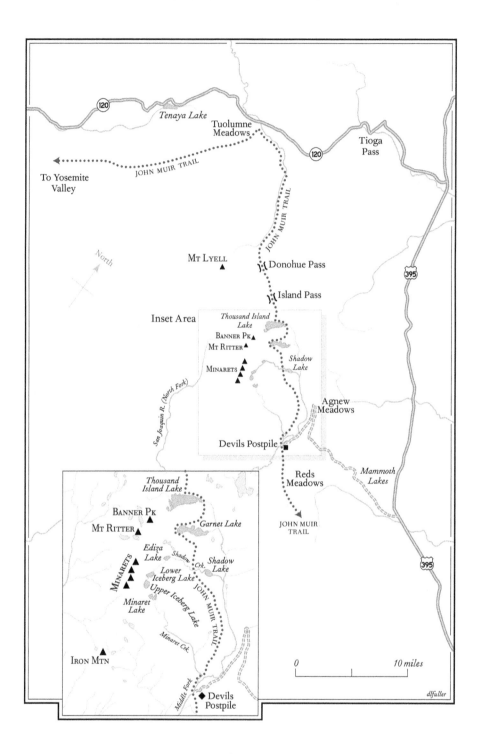

THE RITTER RANGE WITH THE MINARETS AND THE GREATER REGION
(John Muir Trail is shown as it existed in 1933)

Valley, and they followed its developments continuously. It was a high-voltage headline—a bachelor lawyer, son of a prominent family, missing during a daring solo expedition. The authorities, the press reported, conjectured that Starr had become injured and expressed hope that he was still alive.[28]

A patrol found Starr's car at Agnew Meadows, then as now a trail head and pack station between Mammoth Lakes and the Minarets. Not long after, the party came upon his camp along Shadow Creek in a wooded flat just below Ediza Lake in the Ritter Range, a three-hour walk from Agnew Meadows. Peter's name was on his camp outfit and in a notebook. There was no sign of Peter himself and no sign of any foul play. At about 7:00 P.M. on the fourteenth, search officials notified the Starr family by wire about these discoveries.

Curiously, it was revealed that two miners living a hundred yards up Shadow Creek had noticed the abandoned camp more than a week before, and that they apparently had reported the deserted site several times to unknown persons. The abandoned camp had been common knowledge around Agnew Meadows. For unexplained reasons, however, no investigation had been made. The appearance of the campsite gave every indication that Peter had left for a day hike or climb and had failed to return. Given the miners' report, more than a week had been lost.[29]

Mt. Ritter (left) and Banner Peak from Volcanic Ridge.
Photograph by Walter A. Starr, Sr., from a July 1937
trip to the Minarets with Ansel Adams. From the collection
of Walter A. Starr, Sr.

CHAPTER 3

The Ritter Range and The Minarets

The Ritter Range and the Minarets are crown jewels in the Sierra. Like the range of which they are part, these mountains run northwest to southeast. The town closest to them is Mammoth Lakes, twelve air miles to the east. Devils Postpile National Monument is eight miles to the east-southeast. Agnew Meadows, a short drive from Mammoth Lakes, is the nearest trailhead (see the map and figures on pages 34 and 36).

Unlike some taller summits, such as Mt. Whitney, barely standing above the surrounding peaks, the Ritter Range, like Mt. Shasta in California and the Grand Teton range in Wyoming, soars dramatically above its neighbors. At the northwest end of the Ritter Range is Banner Peak (12,945 feet). Immediately to its southwest is Mt. Ritter (13,157 feet), the tallest peak in the range and the highest point in the northern Sierra.[30] Alone, each is prominent. But a saddle joins the two, and so scenic is this ensemble that the pinnacles are customarily referred to as a unit: "Ritter and Banner." No other pair of peaks in the Sierra has so distinctive a shared personality.

Continuing to the southeast is the jagged crest of the Minarets, a two-mile-long, serrated set of black teeth pointing skyward, a thousand feet lower on average than Ritter and Banner, but stunningly magnificent. The various crags within the Minarets were at first known only by number—First Minaret, Second Minaret, and so on—but they gradually acquired non-numerical designations, usually the name of one of the climbers making the first ascent of the particular crag—Clyde Minaret, Michael Minaret, and others.

The entire Ritter Range is dark metamorphic rock, the remnants of an ancient mountain that, unlike most pre-existing formations in the Sierra,

EAST FACE OF THE MINARETS FROM SHADOW CREEK
Drawn by Leland Curtis

THE MINARETS, FROM MINARET CREEK
Drawn by Leland Curtis

survived the powerful upthrust of the light gray Sierra block and at least two ice ages. Spectacular, the Ritter Range was originally included within the boundaries of Yosemite National Park when it was established in 1890, as its southeast corner. Peter Starr himself was clearly impressed with the spot:

> Mt. Ritter and Banner Peak are among the noblest of the Sierra in my opinion. The main crest in this part of the Sierra has been so cut down and broken up that the Ritter Range, paralleling the crest to the west, becomes the real High Sierra in this region. The peaks of Ritter, Banner and the marvelous Minarets rise more as an individual mountain range from lower surroundings than just as peaks along the summit of a crest. This gives them a character and boldness not to be found in other Sierran peaks. Ritter is the dominating peak of the group and the highest summit between Mt. Abbot, far to the south, and Mt. Shasta. Its dark, rectangular, sheer face rises directly west, and almost out of Lake Ediza. Banner, graceful in shape, rises at the head of Garnet and Thousand Island Lakes.[31]

Postcard photograph of the Minarets showing Michael Minaret to the left of Clyde Minaret from the photo collection of Walter A. Starr, Sr. Photograph by Stephen H. Willard.

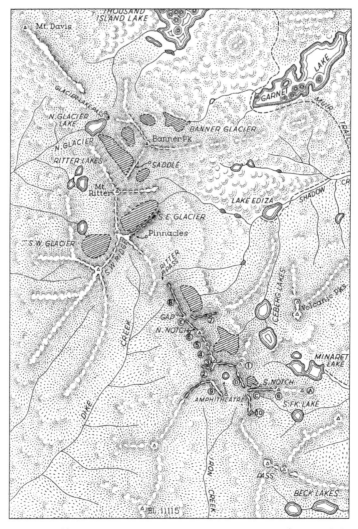

Prepared by *W. A. Starr*   Drawn by *W. B. Wheeler*

MAP OF THE RITTER RANGE, SIERRA NEVADA

1. Clyde Minaret	4. Rice Minaret	7. Leonard Minaret	10. Starr Minaret
2. Michael Minaret	5. Bedayan Minaret	8. Waller Minaret	11. Volcanic Peaks
3. Eichorn Minaret	6. Dawson Minaret	9. Adams Minaret	E. Jensen Minaret

Prepared by Walter A. Starr, Sr., in 1938, this map labelled Michael's Notch as "N. Notch" and labelled the broad U-Notch as the "Gap." As reproduced here, some of the lettered landmarks are omitted from the legend. The map was published in Mr. Starr's edition of the Climber's Guide in the Sierra Club Bulletin in 1938.

*This photograph by Peter Starr was similar to the last image found in his
camera at his Ediza camp. Starr made this image on a long mule trip from
Dusy Basin to Agnew Pass in late season in 1931 or earlier. Clyde Minaret is
on the left; Michael's Notch is in the center; the broad U-Notch is above the
snow field on the right; South Notch is just out of view to the left.*

At least two glacial ages carved up the range and polished its basins. Ediza
Lake (9,272 feet) lies at the center of one basin, flanked on the west by Ritter
and the Minarets, and flowing down from them, by two parallel ridges (the
one on the south called Volcanic Ridge and that on the north called Nydiver
Ridge). In between, Ediza Lake collects the runoff and channels it into a cascade called Shadow Creek that tumbles 1,200 feet down to the Middle Fork of
the San Joaquin River.

Starr's camp was in a wooded flat below Ediza on the north side of
Shadow Creek, a hundred yards east of Nydiver Creek, just west of the sharp

DAWSON MINARET

CLYDE MINARET

MICHAEL'S NOTCH

MINARET PASS

LEONARD MINARET

SOUTH NOTCH

U-SHAPED NOTCH

WALLER MINARET

LOWER-ICEBERG LAKE

*The Minarets and Ediza Lake (in lower left foreground) from Nydiver Ridge
(looking south by southwest). Photograph by William Alsup.*

notch in the trail. It is a pretty spot, shaded by lodgepole pines, softened by fallen needles, and calmed by the stream over which, in the distance, rise the Minarets.

Many breaths have been stolen at Ediza. At the turning of the last uphill stretch of the Shadow Lake Trail, the entire basin bursts into view, having been hidden in stages most of the way up. In the foreground is Ediza's brilliant blue, bordered by green and gray. On the far side of the lake, a half mile away, an upland meadow melds into a series of velvet berms. They rise gradually at first, then ever more steeply, culminating in glaciated bluffs and finally in the vertical heights. On the far left is Clyde Minaret, the highest of that formation (12,281 feet), and on the far right is Banner Peak. Towering above all, Mt. Ritter dominates the center-right and looms large over the lake.

The main line of the Minarets stretches from Clyde to Ritter. Hidden (on the left) behind the primary ridge of Minarets, offset just to its west, is Michael Minaret (12,276 feet), the second highest of the group.[32] All about Ediza, the granite shows red, then green, then red again, for the region has mineral deposits. Up higher, however, the ancient rock is dark. Commencing on the right side of the lake and stretching well upward on the ridge and toward Mt. Ritter is perhaps the Sierra's largest stand of mountain hemlocks, an evergreen forest of majestic "floppy tops." Even in late summer, water tumbles from the perpetual glaciers buried high on the Minarets and Mt. Ritter. "Sublime" is the adjective the nineteenth-century explorers would have applied.

The next lake beyond Ediza is Iceberg Lake, so named for the icebergs that linger there well into summer. In the 1930s (and even today), it was known as Lower Iceberg Lake and that name is used here. Lower Iceberg Lake, whose runoff pours into Ediza Lake, is a mile farther southward, on a direct line between Ediza and Clyde Minaret. Rising immediately south of Lower Iceberg Lake is a wall of granite, ice, and scree, at the top of which is "Minaret Pass," a name that inexplicably has never made it on the official map.[33] Beyond the lip of Minaret Pass rests a yet higher lake, one that was called Upper Iceberg Lake in the 1930s. Though now designated Cecile Lake

Upper Iceberg Lake, looking south. Peter Starr took this photograph in July 1932.
A year later, on August 2, 1933, he bivouacked at this lake before approaching
Michael Minaret via the South Notch.

on the map, it will be referred to here by its former name. Upper Iceberg Lake
drains into Lower Iceberg Lake by way of a stream that pours over the lip and
down the scree and rock.

Mt. Ritter was named in 1864 for Karl Ritter, a German geographer, by
the California Geological Survey, which over the course of its explorations
was responsible for naming most of the prominent peaks in the Sierra. In 1872,
John Muir made the first ascent of Mt. Ritter. Muir's gripping account of the
adventure, including the description of his paralysis brought on by fear on the
vertical rock, is a favorite in Sierra mountaineering literature.[34]

Banner Peak, Ritter's neighbor and an easier climb, was named for the
snow banners that often sail from its summit. The Minarets owe their name to
Clarence King, a member of the Brewer field party and author of *Mountaineer-*

ing in the Sierra Nevada (1872). In 1866, Clarence King and James Gardiner, both on assignment from the California Geological Survey to set the boundaries of the Yosemite Grant of 1864, made the first ascent of Mt. Clark in the Yosemite backcountry (to the west of the Minarets). At the summit, they marveled at the eastern skyline. Mt. Ritter rose even higher than Mt. Clark, and next to Ritter they observed fantastic crags. Gardiner wrote in his journal: "These granite spires in sharpness far surpass anything I have seen in the Sierra. King names them the Minarets."[35]

Mystery, however, shrouds the naming of Ediza Lake. It is remarkable in light of the lake's beauty that no "place name" clues appear in the history books. It is not even known when the name "Ediza" was attached. The Annual Report of the State Mineralogist in 1893 referred to the location as "Little Shadow Lake." The first government map to include the name Ediza Lake was the 1953 Devils Postpile Quadrangle. But as early as 1922, "Edisa Lake" was described in a Yosemite National Park report, and "Ediza Lake" was referenced in 1924 in an account of the first recorded ascent in the Minarets.[36] By 1933, "Ediza" and "Adisa" were interchangeably established.

Although this region was originally the southeast corner of Yosemite National Park, Congress removed it from the park and opened it to mining in 1905, when its tungsten and other ore deposits were much sought. Miners had been prospecting there since at least 1879.[37] The mining interests never struck a rich vein, but the prospectors would not give up.

Once such miner who oversaw a series of claims in the Minarets, David Nydiver, chiseled the Shadow Creek Trail from Agnew Meadows to Ediza Lake no later than the 1920s. In 1929, with the hopes of generating power, his engineers proposed a dam at Ediza that would have raised its level fifty feet. The market crash of 1929 wiped out that scheme. A quarter of a mile below the lake, on a little flat at 9,100 feet, Nydiver constructed a cabin.[38] This was the residence of the miners, associates of Nydiver, who noted that Starr's nearby camp had been abandoned.

In September 1922, Yosemite officials Ansel F. Hall, park naturalist, and

Peter Starr took this late season photograph from Shadow Lake, probably around 1930. The southeast glacier of Mt. Ritter is prominent to the left of Mt. Ritter.

E. C. Solinski, park forester, "examined the mountainous area south and east of Yosemite National Park . . . to determine which part of it, if any, is of premier value from a recreational standpoint, and should, therefore, be included in the Park." Of Ediza Lake, Hall remarked: "Scenically, I should place this lake above all others in the region, with the possible exception of [Lower] Iceberg Lake. To the southwestward the spires of the Minarets tower imposingly above their glaciers and just north of them rise the majestic summits of Banner Peak and Mt. Ritter, two of the highest and most rugged summits on the northern Sierra. Southward, the crags of Volcanic Ridge seem to close in the great Amphitheater with their flanks of colorful rock." Of the hemlock forest, scattered along the north side of the basin, he said, "I have never seen finer stands of this graceful conifer." That assessment still holds valid today. The two men recommended re-inclusion of the Ritter-Banner area into Yosemite National Park, a clarion call that still echoes through generations.[39]

Norman Clyde took this photograph from the summit of Mt. Ritter looking down the Minarets. Clyde and Michael Minarets reach skyward at the far end. Clyde gave this print to Glen Dawson.

CHAPTER 4

Michael and Clyde Minarets

P eter Starr knew, we can be sure, that the first recorded ascent in
the Minarets was by Charles Michael, whose tale the missing man
would have read many times over in the *Sierra Club Bulletin*.[40] In
its own way, that original climb bears upon Starr's story. Charles and Enid
Michael (the assistant postmaster in Yosemite and a Pasadena school teacher,
respectively) had met on a Sierra Club hiking trip, then married in Yosemite. He studied birds, she flowers. They spent a lifetime together in the Sierra
Nevada.[41] In 1923, the couple was living in Yosemite Valley.

In September of that year, the Michaels left Tuolumne Meadows and
headed south over Donohue and Island Passes to the Minarets. Charles and
Enid set up camp near a grove of hemlocks by Ediza Lake. Climbing westward toward the ragged crest of the Minarets, they found a chimney that
offered good handholds and footholds, and led to a cleft in the crest line. (By
1933, this gap had become known as "Michael's Notch," although today it is
also called North Notch; it would serve as an important passageway in the
search for Peter Starr.)

A "stiff climb," Charles wrote, but it was stiffer going down the other
side. On the descent, the husband was prepared to give up and to return to
camp. His climbing partner, however, would not yield, and she found the way
down. Once at the base of the Minarets, the couple moved south, studying
each chimney. They "came to a very narrow chute which appeared to lead
straight to the skyline directly north of the main pinnacle." Up it they went,
believing it would lead to the top of the highest Minaret. They overcame
one difficulty after another until they reached a point where, finally, Charles

"could not bear to see Mrs. Michael take such a chance." She waited under a large slab lodged in the chimney, but urged him on.

At the top of the chimney, another boulder "was jammed in such a way as to leave a portal," or, as Steve Roper described it at the end of the century, "a narrow, thirty-foot-high window at the top of Michael's chimney."[42] This notch became known as "The Portal." There were still one hundred yards of vertical rock to go, which Michael called "the most difficult three hundred feet that I ever had the pleasure of climbing."

The Portal. Photograph by Glen Dawson.

He built "ducks"—markers made of hand-sized, flattish rocks balanced one on another so that, in silhouette, they resemble the profile of a duck—to find his way back:

> Knowing that handhold and footholds seem to be missing, and that the return route never looks the same, I was careful to mark the upward route with ducks. This precaution meant that every time I had to retrace my steps it was necessary to pick up the misleading ducks.[43]

At the summit, the most dramatic vista was of the Minarets themselves:

> The unique view is the one to the north. The highest point of the Minarets lies at the extreme southern end, and looking north one gets a close-up view of the whole wild jumble of peaks that forms the crest of the mountain. A double row of cathedral spires for the distance of a mile would give one a good idea of how the Minarets look when viewed from this point.

It was a "simple matter" to follow his markers back to Mrs. Michael and thence to camp. The Michaels believed that Charles had climbed the highest pinnacle in the group, which was later named Michael Minaret (12,276 feet). It turned out, however, that another spire close by was even loftier, though barely so.[44]

✳   ✳   ✳

The highest minaret is Clyde Minaret (12,281 feet), named for Norman Clyde, who first ascended it in 1928. It is five feet higher than Michael Minaret. From the east at Ediza Lake, Clyde Minaret appears as the massive ruin on the far left, standing guard over Minaret Pass. From the same perspective, Clyde's 1928 route to the top is visible. Clyde clambered up to Upper Iceberg Lake to begin the climb. From there, he mounted the glacier at the north base of the minaret, climbed to its head, crossed over to the rocks, and scrambled up chutes and ribs to the north summit ridge. He then followed the summit ridge left to the top.

On the summit, Norman Clyde penciled his name and the date on a scrap of newsprint about the size of a pocket knife. That scrap was eventually gathered up by the Sierra Club and later transferred, with other Sierra summit signatures, to the Bancroft Library at the University of California at Berkeley, where it now resides among other rare documents and manuscripts.[45]

By universal acclaim, Norman Clyde was the most accomplished mountaineer in Sierra history. He was born in 1885 in Philadelphia, graduated from Geneva College, migrated to California around 1911, married in 1915, and lost his wife to tuberculosis only four years later. In 1924, he became a teacher and principal of the high school in Independence, California.

On Halloween in 1928, Clyde learned that a group of his high school students planned a prank on the school facilities. He hid on campus. When the youths appeared, he confronted them. When they persisted, he fired a pistol shot and they departed. The parents of the students learned of the incident,

and tried to have Clyde arrested for attempted murder. The sheriff declined
on the ground that if Clyde had intended to kill, he would have, since Clyde
was the best shot in the county. The parents did succeed in forcing Clyde's
resignation. That principal/teacher position turned out to be Clyde's last full-
time job.[46]

Clyde, who was already an avid Sierra climber (he made his first ascent in
the range in 1914), devoted most of his new-found free time to mountaineering. At the time he lost his job, Clyde had made forty-six first ascents of Sierra
peaks (not just new routes); by the end of July 1933, that number had grown
to eighty-two. When the seasons allowed, Clyde resided in the Sierra itself,
gypsy-like, in various solo camps hidden off the trail. During winter, he usually occupied a caretaker cabin at Glacier Lodge or at Parchers Camp, once
they closed for the season.[47]

Without regular employment, Clyde suffered financially. He earned
money by selling magazine articles about alpine adventures, by guiding mountaineering clients, and by helping the Sierra Club with its annual High Trips.
His superb memory for minute details of climbing routes (he could recount
step-by-step an ascent sequence, even years later) proved invaluable in the
development of his many articles. He guided the alpinist Julie Mortimer to the
summit of Clyde Minaret in August 1931, the first ascent by a female of any of
the Minarets.[48] It was on this occasion that Clyde left the "register" described
in the introduction to this book on the summit—a rectangle of cardboard
from a Kodak film box with his signature and those of Julie Mortimer and two
other women.

Norman Clyde developed a reputation as a mountain character. Known
for his trademark wide-brimmed Stetson campaign hat with its rear brace band
pulled tight, he was jut-jawed, blue-eyed, ruddy, and strong. Clyde was vari-
ously described as brave, careful, methodical, stubborn, opinionated, stern and
temperamental, sometimes sour, sometimes morose, sometimes very short-
tempered. He believed in doing it right or not at all, and had strong views on
what was right.[49]

Although weighing only 165 pounds and standing five foot nine inches, Clyde hefted a huge pack, weighing upwards of ninety pounds. Besides the usual gear, Clyde carried classic literature, multiple cameras, firewood, pistols, binoculars, even a small anvil to mend his boots. He routinely packed a rope and ice-axe. Usually climbing solo, he used the former to "rope down" on the descent, the latter for ice and snow.[50] David Brower, whose brilliant career was devoted to conservation causes, long ago called Clyde "the pack that walks like a man." And Clyde almost always walked—he did not ride, saying, "I can carry a mule faster than he can carry me."[51]

Peter Starr admired Norman Clyde, having seen so many of Clyde's entries in mountain registers. Starr wrote:

> The ascent of the North Palisade from the glacier on the Owens Valley side is a sporting climb, as far as I know [1928]. This climb has been accomplished only by that indefatigable mountaineer Norman Clyde. It is amusing to compare Clyde's brief and modest account of his very difficult ascent appearing in the register with the lengthy and exhilarated accounts of some of the parties who made the ascent by the route I have described.[52]

Clyde knew Starr the same way. In the register for Middle Palisade, the signature of Walter A. Starr, Jr., in 1930 is followed immediately by those of Norman Clyde from 1930 and 1933. The two never met, however, contrary to lore.

Clyde was renowned for his search-and-rescue abilities. Through 1933, he had found the bodies of three lost hikers and climbers. On a Sierra Club High Trip in the southern Sierra in 1927, a young man tried to climb the Black Kaweah alone, secretly, and against orders. When he did not return, a search party was launched. A paid assistant for the outing, Clyde joined the search and found the young man dead in the cirque between the Red and Black Kaweahs.[53] With his vast knowledge of the Sierra, Clyde had at least twice more located other individuals who had become lost or injured in the mountains.

Now, Peter Starr was missing in the Minarets. Straight away, they called for Norman Clyde. Chief Ranger Allie Robinson wrote the following note to Clyde on Glacier Lodge stationery:

> Dear Norman,
>
> Francis Farquhar called me on the phone from San Francisco last night. Gave me orders to get you and send you to L. A. Camp at Mammoth to search for man by the name of Walter Starr. His car was located at Agnews Meadows, his camp at Adiza Lake. Jules Eichorn and Glen Dawson will also be there.
>
> You can find out all about it from Kellog at L. A. Camp. The man's that is lost is Walter Starr. His father and Jules will be at L. A. Camp today. Father will pay all expenses and wages. They need you very much. Be sure to go.
>
> Allie W. Robinson.[54]

Clyde Minaret from Michael Minaret, 1931.
Photograph by Glen Dawson.

*Aerial photographs of the Minarets taken by Francis Farquhar during the
search for Walter A. Starr, Jr., August 15 and 16, 1933.*

CHAPTER 5

Eichorn and Dawson

The Starr family's anxiety mounted with each day their son failed to return. On the morning of Monday, August 14, Walter Starr contacted Peter's senior at the San Francisco law firm, a tax lawyer named Vincent Butler, who told him that Peter's office was dark and there had been no word from him. Mr. Starr then called the authorities. All involved realized that real mountaineers were desperately needed to search the granite heights. Butler arranged an immediate lunch with the Sierra Club president, Francis Farquhar, at the Bohemian Club in San Francisco.

Francis Farquhar was a prominent certified public accountant in San Francisco. In about 1920, when he climbed in the Palisades, Farquhar fell in love with the "Range of Light," then joined the Sierra Club and tirelessly worked his way up to be its president. In 1931, he organized a climbing school in conjunction with the Sierra Club's annual High Trip. As a result, Farquhar was acquainted with Clyde and all the exuberant young climbers of the Sierra.

It is often said that to get something done, it is best to give the job to the busiest person around; that person is usually the one most organized to accomplish things. Farquhar exemplified that paradox. He was an active citizen who made prodigious contributions to the public good. He enjoyed widely varied interests, friends, and connections, and maintained a relentless business and social calendar. He knew the Sierra by heart. He had personal contacts at nearly every ranger station in the mountains. By sheer dint of industry and passion, Farquhar had organized and positioned himself to assist with practically any situation from Yosemite to Sequoia.

In the quiet of the Bohemian Club, Farquhar listened as his companions told their tale with "great anxiety." As Farquhar grasped the chronology, he became alarmed by the lapse of time. Farquhar's analysis of the situation was both immediate and succinct: If Peter Starr were still alive after so much time, he had to be injured, unable to move, and near water. Though food and clothing would have been important in such circumstances, water was essential. If the searchers acted on the assumption that Starr was still alive, the only assumption that mattered, they had to begin immediately to search near lakes, creeks, glaciers, and snow fields.[55]

Farquhar swung into action. While Butler arranged for a biplane owned by Standard Oil Company (the largest client of the law firm) to be readied at the Presidio Airfield in San Francisco, Farquhar made preparations to leave on short notice. At a dinner party that evening, word came to Farquhar that Starr's camp had been found near Ediza Lake. This development was key because it strongly suggested that Peter was missing in the Minarets.

Early the next morning, the biplane left on its search mission with Farquhar in the rear, open seat, outfitted with flying goggles and camera. Throughout the daylight hours of August 15 and 16, the biplane criss-crossed the Ritter Range. Farquhar carefully studied watercourses, lakes, glaciers, and snow fields, the likely locations where Starr might still be clinging to life. Once when they flew close to the wall of the Minarets they were hit by a down draft. As they pulled higher, Farquhar strained to see any signal from Starr, but was disappointed. He took aerial photographs (see pages 52 and 55). This reconaissance effort was the first aerial search in the Sierra Nevada.[56]

Before departing for the mountains, Farquhar sought the assistance of Glen Dawson and Jules Eichorn, both twenty-one years old, who had distinguished themselves as mountain climbers during the Sierra Club's annual outings. On August 14 at 3:28 P.M., Farquhar sent a Western Union telegram to Dawson in Los Angeles. The wire read: "May need your assistance on search party for Walter Starr Junior reported missing in Sierra STOP Endeavoring locate his car and if found want you to join Clyde and Jules some point east

Aerial photograph of the Minarets taken by Francis Farquhar during the search for Walter A. Starr, Jr., August 15 and 16, 1933. Clyde Minaret is in the center, and South Notch is in the lower left.

side STOP Please wire me that you are holding yourself in readiness for short notice."[57] He telephoned Jules Eichorn in San Francisco with the same message.

Both Eichorn and Dawson had just returned from a month on the 1933 Sierra Club High Trip. They dropped everything, however, and stood by for duty—Dawson in Los Angeles and Eichorn in San Francisco. Farquhar also reached Chief Ranger Douglas Robinson of the U.S. Forest Service in Mammoth Lakes and asked him to track down Norman Clyde and send him to Ediza, as recounted above. After Starr's car and camp were located on August 14, Farquhar broke away from his dinner party to dispatch to the scene two groups of climbers—one from Los Angeles and the other from Piedmont. Glen Dawson and a climbing friend he recruited, Richard Jones, embarked from the south.[58] To the north, a group assembled at the Starr home, then departed. It included Jules Eichorn, Walter A. Starr, Sr., Allan Starr (Peter's brother), and three of Peter's friends.

Jules Eichorn and Glen Dawson were emblematic of a golden chapter in Sierra mountaineering history. Though from opposite ends of the state, the pair developed into one of the most prominent climbing teams in California, their names fused as solidly as Ritter and Banner. Now at age twenty-one, they were cast as leading characters in the dramatic search for Peter Starr.

Eichorn was born in 1912, the son of German immigrants. Eichorn's father and uncle ran a tailor shop in San Francisco. His mother took in boarders. Both parents were musically inclined, and they began piano lessons for Eichorn at age eleven. In 1925, when he was thirteen, they found him a new piano teacher—a twenty-three-year-old Ansel Adams. To pay for his lessons, Eichorn worked as Adams' photographic assistant, sometimes washing prints in the bathtub. At age fifteen, Eichorn won second place in the San Francisco Piano Contest, beating out over one hundred other contestants.

In 1927, Adams persuaded Eichorn's parents that young Jules should accompany him on the annual Sierra Club High Trip, for which Adams was then the camp master. The trips typically lasted a month, included two hundred or so campers, a long pack train, cooks, packers, guides, and leaders. Huge iron stoves, cooking pots, food, and other gear were transported, as the expedition moved from camp to camp. Such was the exuberant scale of mountain recreation in the era. Participants hiked, swam, sang, and ate—and quite a number climbed. Mountaineers returned from the very highest altitudes with sprigs of polemonium (the rare alpine wildflower known as sky pilot) pinned to their caps. Eichorn made his first mountain ascent—of Alta Peak—on that 1927 trip, in the company of Adams. Eichorn was fifteen.[59]

During that outing, Eichorn met Glen Dawson, who was the same age but from Los Angeles. Glen was the son of Ernest Dawson, a mountaineer and founder of Dawson's Book Shop, a rare book store still serving collectors from its West Los Angeles stacks. Eichorn and Dawson went up Mt. Kaweah with Adams. It was the first time that Eichorn and Dawson climbed together. It was

Jules Eichorn, 1931. Photograph by Glen Dawson.

the same Sierra Club trip that resulted in the death of the young man on Black Kaweah. Eichorn and Dawson aided in the search, and in that loose sense made their first climb with Norman Clyde. Although Dawson had previously and briefly met Clyde through his father,[60] the 1927 outing was Eichorn's first real introduction to the Sierra legend (and, as it happened, to Farquhar).

The 1928 outing took participants to Canada, but neither youngster went along. The budding climbers made up for lost time on the 1929 High Trip. Eichorn scaled Mounts Ritter and Ban-

*Glen Dawson circa 1933.
Photograph by Ansel Adams, from the
collection of Glen Dawson.*

ner, while Dawson climbed, among other things, Clyde Minaret via a new, all-rock route. Dawson left a note at the top of Clyde Minaret stating that they had "found Norman Clyde's record of June 28, 1928, lying loose, written on newspaper scraps."[61] Thanks to Dawson, who put it in the register can, that artifact is now safe, if severely wrinkled, in the Bancroft Library. Although Dawson and Eichorn did not make ascents together that summer, they regularly compared mountaineering notes and became better friends, making arrangements to climb as a team the following year.

The next summer (1930), Eichorn again drove over from San Francisco with Ansel Adams for another High Trip.[62] As agreed, Eichorn met Dawson, and they then began a famous series of climbs together. The route of the 1930 outing can be traced by their successive ascents: Red and White, Abbot, Bear Creek Spire, Gabb, Darwin, The Hermit, McGee, Mendel, Goddard, Devils Crags, Woodward, Middle Palisade (from the southwest), Sill, North Palisade, Polemonium, Winchell, and Agassiz Needle. Theirs was a phenomenal achievement.

Jules Eichorn and Walter "Bubs" Brem, Jr., on Michael's Minaret, 1931.
Photograph by Glen Dawson.

Still more astounding was 1931, a season that many believe was the zenith of early mountaineering in the Sierra Nevada. Young Eichorn and Dawson were sensational as the 1931 outing party wandered along the eastern Yosemite wilderness, beginning and ending in Tuolumne Meadows. The pair (usually together with Walter "Bubs" Brem, Jr., another youngster) climbed many peaks, several of them in the Minarets.

*Near the top of Clyde Minaret looking west to Michael Minaret and Third Minaret
(Eichorn Minaret), 1931. Photograph by Glen Dawson.*

On July 31, as the main group prepared to move to Garnet Lake (two
miles north of Ediza), the climbers went ahead to the Minarets, crossing over
them to the west side. They first climbed Michael Minaret and left a note at the
top, stating that they had come "via Michael's chimney" and that "the peak
to the east" [Clyde Minaret] was higher. Dropping back down to The Portal,
they then crossed over to the summit of what was then called Third Minaret
(but soon renamed Eichorn Minaret). Finally, they worked up and down a
jagged arete to Clyde Minaret. No one had ever before mounted two of the
Minarets in a single day, much less three, and this youthful party had navi-
gated the treacherous traverse between them as well!

On the last pinnacle, Glen Dawson left a note: "This is the highest Minaret, we used hand level."[63] (A hand level was a tool with a bubble and mirror
that told the user when the sighting tube was level.) They returned to camp
via the front (east) side of Clyde Minaret, after a fourteen-hour day. This

achievement was later chronicled by Dawson in the *Sierra Club Bulletin*,[64] and Starr must have studied it before his own 1933 exploration.[65]

Soon after, Robert Underhill joined the 1931 High Trip. Underhill was a professor at Harvard and perhaps the most famous American alpinist of the time. Farquhar had persuaded Underhill to organize an informal climbing school and teach modern rope-management techniques for the 1931 outing. The rope, Underhill emphasized, was to be used for safety, not as an aid in climbing. He contended that through safety, more difficult climbs could be attempted. On August 3, utilizing ropes for protection, Underhill and Eichorn pioneered a new route up the steep east face of Mt. Banner (at the end of Garnet Lake).

Palisade Climbing School, 1931.
Back row, left to right: Francis Farquhar, Bestor Robinson, Glen Dawson, Neil Wilson,
and Lewis Clark. Front row, left to right: Robert Underhill, Norman Clyde, Jules
Eichorn, and Elmer Collett. Photograph courtesy of Glen Dawson.

Richard M. Jones and Glen Dawson.
Photograph by Ruth Dyer Mendenhall, 1934,
from the collection of Glen Dawson.

Immediately following the High Trip, Underhill continued his climbing lessons in the Palisades region with eight students from the outing and Norman Clyde. This was the first real climbing Eichorn and Dawson got to do with Clyde. On August 9, they ascended the North Palisade. On August 11, Underhill, Clyde, Eichorn, and Dawson forged a new route up the north face of Temple Crag.

On August 13, the group scaled a peak neighboring North Palisade. As Eichorn and Dawson climbed the difficult summit monolith, an electrical storm flashed all about them. Sparks flew off Eichorn's fingers and ice axe, prompting the party to retreat. Eichorn was the last off the summit. As he left, a tremendous explosion immobilized him. It took him some time to determine that he was still alive. Once the group found crude shelter under an overhang, Farquhar proposed, successfully as it turned out, that the precipice be named Thunderbolt Peak.[66]

The students' final exam was their attempt of a first ascent of the east face of Mt. Whitney, at the southern anchor of the Sierra chain. The route started at East Face Lake and was nearly vertical. There were two climbers and two

Glen Dawson on Finger Rocks, 1931, from the collection of
Glen Dawson.

ropes. Underhill teamed with Dawson, and Clyde with Eichorn. The elder men let the two nineteen-year-olds lead most of the way up. At the summit they were met by an ecstatic Farquhar, who had ascended by a different route, and by an astounded troop of boy scouts. They passed their final exam.

What did Eichorn, Dawson, and these youngsters talk about around the campfire? By this point, Eichorn and Dawson had graduated from high school.

[63]

Eichorn was teaching music in San Francisco to earn his way, and Dawson was a student at UCLA. According to Dawson (commenting in 1998 at age eighty-six) all the young men thought and conversed about was climbing and the outdoor life, and they discussed the best ascent routes, the best knapsack menus, and fishing—pretty tame subject matter.[67]

The 1932 and 1933 High Trips generated more legend. One example suffices. In 1933, Eichorn and Dawson topped three separate crags of the Devils Crags in two days with climber Ted Waller. On one of the days, a tremendous storm caught all three high on the Kings Canyon rock, as Dawson later recalled:

> In a few moments the water had increased from a trickle which we could catch in our cups to a torrent of alarming proportions. Jules had gone out onto a narrow ledge, where he was soon drenched by water, and, what was more serious, was exposed to falling rocks. The roar of water, the lightning and thunder, and the crashing of avalanches were stupendous, but not very pleasant to us at the time. Soaked with rain and spray, we were so cold that we shook all over every few minutes. We could see snowfields below us blotted out by slowly moving rockslides, and we could see gullies being dug ten feet deep. Individual rocks came down, breaking into pieces on every side. The Devils Crags seemed to be coming apart.
>
> For an hour Jules was forced to stay in an extremely precarious position on a narrow ledge, exposed to falling rocks and threatened with being swept off by the increasing force of the water. At last the storm abated, and Ted was able to pass a rope to Jules and assist him across to our side of the chimney. Slowly we made our way down a few hundred feet of difficult wet rock. It was dusk before we got to timber and a chance to dry out. We tried to get to the Sierra Club camp at Palisades Creek on

Walter "Bubs" Brem, Jr., and Jules Eichorn on Michael Minaret, 1931.
Clyde Minaret is to the left. Photograph by Glen Dawson.

the Middle Fork of Kings River that night, but our exhaustion
was too much even for the promise of food . . . [68]

Decades later, Ted Waller recalled this storm as the worst he ever saw in the
Sierra. After Jules was trapped on the ledge, Waller and Dawson were unable
to see him because so much debris was falling down with the rain. The storm
lasted almost an hour. They bivouacked, and the next morning dragged themselves back into camp, just as Clyde was about to lead a rescue party out to
find them.[69]

The 1933 High Trip members marched triumphantly out of the Sierra at
South Lake, a few miles above Bishop, the largest town in the Owens Valley, on Saturday, August 5. Eichorn and Dawson, each twenty-one years old,
parted without a clue that trouble was afoot in the Minarets to the north. Now,
a week later, under a starlit sky, they were heading back to timberline.[70]

CHAPTER 6

Ediza Base Camp

Through the night the two caravans closed on their destination. The searchers reported to Chief Ranger Douglas "Allie" Robinson at 7:00 a.m. on August 15 in Mammoth Lakes. Two of Peter's friends from the Bay Area contingent, Lowell Hardy and Whiting Welch, remained with Ranger Robinson at Mammoth Lakes to coordinate the handling of supplies and information, while another friend drove Peter's car home.[71]

Of course, in that era the authorities had no portable radios or helicopters. All supplies and information were carried and delivered on foot or horseback. A twelve-person search party from the Mammoth Lakes area, including Civilian Conservation Corps youth, volunteers, and law enforcement officers, arrived that day at Ediza Lake. With them were packers, mules, horses, cooks, and the support team needed for such an operation.

Mr. Starr, Allan Starr, Jules Eichorn, Glen Dawson, and Dick Jones were driven to Agnew Meadows, where they began their hike to Ediza with two mules carrying gear and supplies; they reached Ediza at 3:00 P.M. As they were hiking in, the biplane carrying Francis Farquhar circled the Ritter Range.[72] Just before they reached Ediza, they passed by Peter's abandoned camp.

After dark on August 15, Norman Clyde and a companion, Oliver Kehrlein, arrived at Ediza on horseback (one of the rare times Clyde rode an animal), having hastened from Glacier Lodge, where they had been exploring the Palisades glaciers. Kehrlein was a Sierra Club regular from Oakland who went on to organize the Sierra Club Base Camp Outings from 1940 to 1957. He happened to be with Clyde when the trouble struck and he joined in. From Mammoth came two other climbers, Douglas Robinson, Jr., the son of Ranger

Allie Robinson, and Lilburn Norris. Altogether, there were about twenty in the search party.[73] It was an assembly of extraordinary talent, arguably the strongest search-and-rescue team ever assembled in Sierra mountaineering history. They set up camp above Ediza Lake near the inlet stream that tumbles down from the Minarets.

Recreating the details of the ensuing search is aided by two published accounts of it. The earliest was a 4½-page summary in the June 1934 issue of the *Sierra Club Bulletin*, edited by Farquhar and based mainly on letters from Clyde and Dawson. A carbon copy of the Dawson letter, written on August 21, 1933, still exists and includes details not mentioned in the *Sierra Club Bulletin*. The complete letter from Clyde has not been located.

The second account, a chapter entitled "The Quest For Walter Starr," was written much later by Clyde and published in the book *Norman Clyde of the Sierra Nevada*, released in 1972. This nine-page account will be referred to simply as *Quest*. Important other material, most of which is now at the Bancroft Library or provided by Dawson and Eichorn, has helped enlarge the details substantially. Apparently, no photographs of the search itself were taken; none is extant—save the aerial photographs taken by Farquhar. Clyde maintained a field notebook, now in the possession of two Norman Clyde scholars in Berkeley. In it, Clyde made an entry for every day of the search. Unfortunately, he wrote down precious few search details, preferring instead to jot phrases about flowers, birds, rocks, trees, and weather, apparently in chronological order, perhaps to help him recreate descriptions more accurately later on.

The entire assembly, including the alpinists, was under the direction of the authorities, but a cooperative division of labor was immediately clear. In *Quest*, Norman Clyde summarized the search strategy as follows:

> Almost undoubtedly Walter Starr had met with mishap some-
> where in this group of mountains, the Ritter Range, and was
> either somewhere on them or in the country lying between them
> and his camp. If killed or seriously injured he was probably

in the mountains, but if he were only crippled he might have attempted to reach camp and, being unable to do so, would be in the lower country. A man with a sprained ankle or broken leg may spend days in going a short distance. The plan of campaign was based on these facts. Those without special mountaineering experience were to comb the area lying between his camp and the base of the Ritter Range. The mountaineers were to search the peaks and spires, a difficult, arduous, and somewhat hazardous undertaking.[74]

Of course, no one knew whether Starr was on the crags at all. He might have drowned in the lake, as one newspaper speculated. He might have been lying helplessly in the hemlock forest or been miles away, unable to move. Several broad possibilities presented themselves. The job of the mountaineers, however, was to devote their energies to the most dangerous possibility, the pinnacles and minarets of the Ritter Range. There was less chance that Starr would survive higher up than if he were in the lower country, but the alpinists were eager to begin if there was even a small likelihood that Peter was still alive.

As noted, Starr's camp was not at Ediza itself but slightly below the lake along Shadow Creek and near the miners' cabin. A packer who supplied the search party from Agnew Meadow later pointed out the location as somewhat below the cabin. He placed it between the trail and Shadow Creek (north of the stream) about one hundred yards below Nydiver Creek and just above a narrow, steep chute in the trail.[75]

In Starr's camp at Ediza, searchers found his ice-axe, his crampons, his Kodak camera and case, and ample food to last several days. He had left no message, though his ascent notes were later uncovered in his gear. His camera was sent to Mammoth Lakes in hopes that developing its film would provide clues to Starr's whereabouts, at least by showing where he had already been.[76]

From his camp, a large number of summits were within range and visible, and Starr might have been attracted to any of them. Six had been previously climbed: Mounts Ritter and Banner, and the Clyde, Michael, Eichorn, and Leonard Minarets.[77] There were as well several unnamed minarets with no recorded ascents. On the other hand, Starr might have gone off on a trail reconnaissance for recordings of mileage, elevations, vistas, and camps, in aid of his guidebook project.

Many questions leapt to mind. Which climbs had Starr already accomplished? Had Starr tried to scale a previously unconquered minaret so that he could affix his name to it? Had he tried a new route up one of the previously-climbed six? Why were his ice-axe and crampons still in camp? Was it because he wasn't climbing at all or because he did not intend to climb on ice? Why was his camera left in camp? Was it because he had a difficult route in mind and did not want the extra weight? "The fact," Dawson wrote in his August 21 letter, that Starr had "left his crampons and ice-axe and camera made other searchers believe [Starr] was not on a high mountain but it only made me believe he was out to do real rock work."[78]

The answers to these and other questions were not forthcoming. The pattern of the soles of Starr's shoes was unknown, for example. Mr. Starr and Whiting Welch "were under the impression" that Starr had been mountaineering in the Minarets before.[79] In fact, Starr had climbed Mt. Banner in 1930, Mt. Ritter in 1929 and 1932, and Clyde Minaret in 1932.[80] Mrs. Stephen Willard, a resident of Mammoth Lakes, had seen Starr at Ediza on the evening of July 30. She reported that Starr said he was going all the way to Kearsarge Pass, at least one hundred miles to the south (and presumably would have come out at Glacier Lodge to re-provision).[81] But his well-provisioned camp indicated that Starr had remained in the immediate region.

The mountaineers decided that they would divide into four search parties the next morning and search the four highest peaks: Clyde and Michael Minarets on the left (south) and Mt. Ritter and Mt. Banner on the right (north). They parceled out the search assignments based upon prior experience on the target peaks, then retired to the music of glacial brooks.

*Mr. Starr took this photograph during his July 1937 trip to
the Minarets with Ansel Adams. He wrote under the image:
"Clyde Minaret (right) and Lake Minaret Spur
(looking N.W.—Lake Minaret lies below)."*

*One of the frames from the film recovered from Peter Starr's camera. He completed
the ascent of Mt. Ritter on July 30, 1933. The author made the print from a
negative found in the basement of the Starr family ranch.*

CHAPTER 7

August 16

The searchers wasted no daylight. Straightaway on August 16, the Ritter party discovered evidence of Starr's movements:

> The climbers were off at 6 A.M. the morning of the 16th. Douglas Robinson, Jr., and Lilburn Norris, of Mammoth, climbed Ritter by a route up the east side of the mountain, pointed out to them as one known to have been taken before by Starr. They succeeded in reaching the summit and found that Starr had registered there on the 31st of July, saying that he had used crampons and ice axe, having crossed the glacier.[82]

The Ritter register—a book with lined pages—now rests at the Bancroft Library at the University of California at Berkeley, along with hundreds of other tattered mountain registers retrieved from the Sierra. It shows that the date of Starr's entry was clearly July 30, not July 31 as reported in the *Sierra Club Bulletin* account reproduced above. This error has been uniformly repeated in all subsequent Sierra Club references on the subject, including guides and mountaineering records.[83] The full note, punctuated and lined as follows, actually read:

> July 30, 1933 Walter A Starr, Jr.
> 3rd ascent—this time de luxe
> with crampons and ice axe via
> glacier from Lake Ediza.[84]

The next entry in the Ritter register was dated August 3, 1933, by a group of five members from a Los Angeles chapter of "Die Naturfreunde," a German hiking club. Then, on August 16, the search party wrote the following passage:

August 16, 1933
D. Robinson, Jr.
Lilburn Norris   Bishop, California

Fairly good climb from Lake Ediza up south-east side of the peak, following a fissure most the way. Had no crampons or ice axe, so could not get on glacier, mostly chimney-sweep work. We came on a hunt for Walter A. Starr, Jr., who has been missing since the first. First Ascent.

The search party observed that Starr had been missing "since the first" (not the seventh, when he was to meet his father at Glacier Lodge) probably because of the miners' report of a vacant camp since about that date. Because the searchers noted the purpose of their visit, subsequent climbers thus were alerted to be on the lookout for signs of Starr and to report any information they might have about him to the authorities. (The meaning of the notation "First Ascent" is unclear. If it was to indicate that Norris and Robinson had made the first ascent by their route, they did not get credit for it in the *Climber's Guide*. It is more likely that they simply meant it was their first ascent.[85])

Back at Ediza, two facts confirmed Starr's safe return from Mt. Ritter. First, his ice axe and crampons were there, the same items he had used to climb the peak, according to his entry. Second, Starr's notes on the ascent were found among his gear, and had obviously been made after his descent.[86] There seemed little reason to focus any longer on Ritter.

As it turned out, most of the photographs from Starr's camera were taken during his Ritter climb, and showed the brightly lit glacier route at various elevations. They are published here for the first time (see pages 72 and 76).

There was no photo from the summit, perhaps because Starr already had such an image. The last two images on the roll show the view from the east shore of Ediza: the lake, the Minarets, and the last evening light on the pinnacles (see page 108). None of the photos, unfortunately, provided any clue that could further narrow the possibilities. None suggested a trip up any other peak that could have eliminated the need to check there.[87]

❋   ❋   ❋

The Mt. Banner contingent of the search party consisted of Mr. Starr and his son Allan. Both son and father had respectable mountaineering résumés. In 1925, Allan and his brother had climbed together in the Palisades.[88] Besides his climb of North Palisade on the 1929 excursion (a difficult task by any standard), Allan also had scaled a few lesser peaks in the Yosemite region.[89] Although neither Mr. Starr nor Allan had ever attempted Banner, it was the least difficult of the four assignments. The Banner party found no sign of Starr:

> W. A. Starr, Sr., and his son Allan Starr climbed Banner, going
> up the southeast side by way of the saddle and down the west
> side, searching the two glaciers, and returning around the north
> and east base of the mountain across the heads of Thousand
> Island and Garnet lakes. It was found that Starr had not regis-
> tered on the summit of Banner.[90]

The Banner summit register (also in the Bancroft Library) is today in poor condition with almost every page in a ragged state. The Starrs' signatures accompany a statement that they had been looking for "Walter A. Starr, Jr. . . . since August 2." The exact phrase can only be conjecture, as part of the page has been torn away, but the date was probably used because of the information provided by the local miners.[91] This entry, too, served to inform subsequent summiters of the special need to report any clues in the matter. It may

One of the frames from the film recovered from Peter Starr's camera, showing the southeast Ritter glacier. The author made this print from a negative found in the basement of the Starr family ranch.

have been that the two search parties agreed to leave such alerts in the registers as they hiked toward Ritter and Banner on their overlapping approaches.

The search must have been excruciating for father and brother. Having lost a week in delay, they had to contend with feelings of guilt and a sense of tragedy as they forced themselves to concentrate on the task at hand. To their credit, they refused to allow others to assume the full risk of the search. If others were going to be in harm's way to help the Starr family, then the Starr family was going to share the burden, too.

❁   ❁   ❁

The Clyde Minaret search party consisted of Clyde and Kehrlein. They scrambled up the glaciated bluffs above Ediza, then worked their way south, with the lake below them and the crags above, scouring the area for any traces of the missing man. Footprints were found, but neither searcher knew the pattern of the soles of the shoes worn by Starr. They soon came to the base of the glacier at Clyde Minaret, the glacier that Clyde had crossed in his first ascent in 1928. Clyde later recalled:

> Leaving the bluffs, we crossed a small but rather steeply pitching glacier to the base of Clyde Minaret and continued up its precipitous north face. More tracks were observed in the decomposed granite on the ledges, but these also were in all likelihood those of another party. Upon reaching the jagged top of the great spire, the signature of Walter Starr was not in the register in the cairn. However, we knew that he did not always sign his name on the top of a mountain, and furthermore there was no pencil in the register can and he might have failed to bring one with him. No evidence of his having been there was discovered.[92]

Clyde and Kehrlein signed a paper in the register can and dated it August 15, 1933. In his accounts, Clyde made no mention of seeing any signs of anyone having climbed on the glacier itself, although it is unlikely that evidence of a person's passage on the snow and ice would have been discernible after two and a half weeks in the sunlight. Clyde continued:

> As we looked out over the mountains an inky mass of clouds was seen advancing from the southwest and another from the northeast. As the top of a pinnacle more than 12,000 feet above the sea is not the most desirable place to encounter an electric storm, we left the summit before we had searched it to our entire satisfaction.[93]

In his field notebook, Clyde wrote the following for August 15:

Approach summit; extensively large dark thunderstorms sweeping from the S.W. to the N.E., another mass approaching from N.E.: hearing reverberating peak of thunder from both; sun still shining in Minarets, look hastily at register, scan notes for 10 or 15 minutes; claps of thunder. Hasten down mountain as heavy dark clouds gather over Ritter and Banner and peak of thunder reverberate but storm from S.W. passes by and other halts at Ritter and Banner, the clouds lowering and swirling about their summits.[94]

In *Quest*, Clyde wrote that "On our way down we zigzagged back and forth, minutely observing every square yard for clues, but none were found."[95] There was, it seems, no sign that Starr had taken Clyde's glacier route, much less that he had come to grief on it. What's more, the ice-climbing gear he would have found extremely helpful for crossing the glacier was found in Starr's camp.

Still, the large crevasse between Clyde Minaret and the glacier itself—called a bergschrund—was a plausible spot to look for Starr. The bergschrund was often twenty or more feet deep, narrow, constantly filling with debris, and slowly grinding up its contents. If Starr had fallen in, he might not have been visible under the debris and, conceivably, might have left no sign of trouble on the surface of the glacier.

Clyde next investigated the "front" of the minaret, i.e., its "northeast face," according to his account:

When we reached the glacier, I swung around a promontory and found a long ledge running across the northeast face of the peak. Knowing the adventurous character of the lost man, I had a strong suspicion that he would attempt this apparently sheer, and so far as we knew, hitherto unscaled front of the mountain. About midway across the latter I came upon a "duck"—a small heap of rocks usually pyramidal in form, erected as a marker to indicate a route followed. Presently I saw another and then a whole line of them leading to the head of a steep chimney on the southeast shoulder of the mountain. The ducks had evidently been constructed no great while before, as some of them were so unstable that they would have toppled over under the first heavy wind. However, it did not seem very likely that Starr would have approached this face from the southeast and we knew that another party, of whose movements we had not been informed, had also been in this vicinity. Later we learned that such a party had recently made an unsuccessful attempt to scale the Minaret by this route.[96]

These observations by Clyde are puzzling in at least two respects. First, he wrote that the "northeast face" of the mountain had not previously been climbed. He surely knew, however, that Dawson had made the ascent in 1929. The *Sierra Club Bulletin* account of the incident indicates that the search party was aware that Starr had climbed the very route himself in 1932. That Clyde believed the northeast face was untried territory is enigmatic.

Second, Clyde mentioned that Starr "did not always sign his name at the top of a mountain." This statement seems contrary to the facts. Starr made solo entries in dozens of summit registers, and Clyde must have seen many of them. Dawson noted that "Starr usually wrote lengthy accounts in registers I have seen."[97] Clyde seems to have inferred that Starr did not always sign registers from the fact that Starr had scaled the same minaret in 1932 and no record of that ascent was found at the summit cairn during Clyde's 1933 search.

Because it was late in the day, Clyde and Kehrlein did not follow the ducks to their conclusion. They started back to camp, pausing to reconnoiter near the outlet of Upper Iceberg Lake. There, Clyde noticed and picked up a strip of bloodstained handkerchief. He conjectured that someone had lost his or her footing on the steep slope coming up from Lower Iceberg Lake and cut a finger on a sharp rock. The men also observed that the small area of grass at

Upper Iceberg Lake near the outlet at Minaret Pass had the faint sign of someone having rested on it. Back at Ediza, they learned that the border pattern on
the handkerchief strip matched the type carried by Starr.[98]

Norman Clyde's findings for the day included a bloodied bandage, the
hint of a resting spot at the highest lake, and rock route markers on the northeast face of Clyde Minaret. But Starr had left no record of having been on top
of the pinnacle. Was this because there had been no pencil in the register can
and because Starr had not been carrying one, as Clyde speculated? There was
the possibility that Starr had fallen into the Clyde bergschrund, the yawn-
ing crevice where the top of the glacier pulled away from the rock, but Clyde
doubted this. He did not doubt, however, that Starr had started up this highest
of the Minarets.

※   ※   ※

The fourth climbing group was the youthful crew of Jules Eichorn,
Glen Dawson, and the latter's friend Richard Jones. They had been assigned
Michael Minaret because Eichorn and Dawson had made the ascent in 1931
and were familiar with the way. The three men followed the Michaels' route
up the long massive ridge that ends at the base of Michael's Notch, then
scrambled through the notch before dropping over to the west side. Dawson
described the climb in a letter to Francis Farquhar:

> On the 16th, Jules, Dick Jones, and I crossed Michael's notch to
> the west side of the Minarets. We climbed a fine high pinnacle
> on the main crest of the Minarets under the impression we were
> climbing Leonard Minaret. We went down a different chute to
> the one we went up.[99]

As it turns out, they did not climb Leonard Minaret, which was located a little
to the north; instead they scaled a spire just south of Michael's Notch, mistak-
ing it for Leonard Minaret. Because this was the first instance the pinnacle had

been topped, it later became known as Dawson Minaret. Once down on the west side, the party proceeded south to the base of Michael Minaret. As Dawson explained, they ascended via a chute different from Michael's:

> We next went up the first chute north of Michael's Wnding evidence of a recent big slide. Near the top of the chute we came across a line of ducks and a half-smoked Chester Weld cigarette . . . We followed the ducks to a point below the two large spires north of Michael Minaret and draining into Michael's chimney.[100]

Here were clear signs of recent climbing activity. The young men did not know whether Starr smoked or his preferred brand if he did. Because the cigarette was found near the top of a chute between Eichorn and Michael Minarets, the searchers scanned the nearby terrain for any other sign of Starr. Large areas of the rock face were hidden from view by ribs, chutes, and other irregularities. Finding and seeing nothing, "Jules and I hurried up Michael Minaret, but found no evidence of anyone having been there since our previous climb with Brem in 1931."[101]

When Eichorn and Dawson were at the summit of the pinnacle, they made their entry in the register directly under their names from two years earlier. No one else had signed the book in between. This suggested that the maker of the rock ducks did not reach the top of Michael Minaret (or inexplicably did not sign its register).

Unlike the Ritter and Banner teams, the Eichorn-Dawson team did not note the purpose of their visit in the register. Evidently, they felt it unlikely that anyone else would soon follow them to the top, given the rigorous climbing required.

Perched at the top, Eichorn and Dawson discussed descending a different way. They considered going down and examining the steep northwest face of Michael Minaret, then connecting eventually with Michael's chute. "Heavy storms made further investigation inadvisable," Dawson noted.[102] The same threat was forcing the Clyde Minaret team off the top as well. The alternate plan would have taken too much time and the wet rock would have been too dangerous. So, retracing their steps, Eichorn and Dawson dropped back to The Portal, went down Michael's chimney (with Jones), and returned to Lake Ediza over the big gap north of Michael's Notch. The team had investigated as many chutes and passes as possible, going up one way and returning another, the only exception being the duplicate route up and down the summit pitch.

Back at Ediza, it was established that Starr smoked Chesterfield cigarettes, the brand that was found.[103] While all the evidence pointed to the fact that Starr had been climbing in the area of the Minarets, there was no trace of Starr at the top of the formation: no cairn and no note.

One unexplored possibility was that Starr had climbed Eichorn Minaret (located immediately adjacent to Michael Minaret), because the ducked route led to both formations. Though there was no visual sign of Starr on Eichorn from several hundred feet away, the searchers had not climbed the pinnacle. Further, the pervasive system of ribs and chutes on Michael and the rest of the Minarets created a vast maze of hidden crevices and irregularities. Starr could have been on Michael or Eichorn—practically anywhere—and been hidden from sight.

That evening, with the silhouette of the Ritter Range carved upon the starlit canopy, the observations of the various teams were analyzed at camp. The Civilian Conservation Corps volunteers and law enforcement officers had found nothing in the lower country. The group agreed that Starr's first climb had been of Mt. Ritter, and despite momentary speculation that Starr had fallen into the bergschrund on Mt. Ritter on his return trip, there was no doubt now that he had returned safely to camp.

Because there was not even a trace placing Starr on Mt. Banner, the group concentrated on the evidence from the Minarets. On the west side of the Minarets, the clues included the cigarette butt, the rock slide, and the ducks near Michael and Eichorn Minarets. On the east side of the Minarets, the leads included the bloodied handkerchief strip, the faint resting place near Upper Iceberg Lake, and the ducks on Clyde Minaret. Complicating the matter, Starr had not signed the register on Michael or Clyde Minaret. His notes at camp gave no indication (after his mention of Mt. Ritter) of his past or future destinations. And there was a sky full of other minarets.

The discussion drifted to the Clyde Minaret bergschrund where Starr might have fallen and been covered by debris. That theory had gained currency in the continuing newspaper coverage, and it conveniently explained why Starr could not be found. Because there was no glacier or bergschrund on the west sides of Michael and Eichorn Minarets, Clyde was also the only location where a bergschrund scenario was possible. Although the relevant clues did not really coalesce to suggest a single, consistent explanation, the finger of suspicion pointed to the Clyde/Michael/Eichorn region, the high southern end of the Minarets. The climbers decided to narrow their search and focus it there. That would be their challenge for the next day.[104]

CHAPTER 8

August 17 and 18

The next morning, Clyde and Kehrlein returned to the region they had explored the previous day. In his account, Clyde described their second visit to the Clyde Minaret:

Haunted by the ducks on the northeast face of Clyde Minaret, Kehrlein and I returned on the following morning to Upper Iceberg Lake. Swinging around to the slope east of it, we selected a vantage point from which the entire northeast face could be readily surveyed with binoculars. An object about a third of the way up the mountain puzzled me. The fact that it was brown indicated that it might be a khaki-clad person, but as the light falling upon it seemed to be diffused through it rather than reflected from it, this inference seemed to be precluded. Having come to the decision that this face of the peak should be thoroughly investigated, we proceeded to climb it. In about half an hour we reached the long ledge. After examining several ducks, I carefully removed the rocks of one of them. Beneath was a tuft of grass the color of which had not faded in the least. This was certain proof that the ducks had been made very recently. As we began to advance up the peak we presently came upon more ducks. Then there was a gap. Evidently the climber was in the habit of putting markers only when he thought that there might be special occasion for them on his return. A little later we reached the object which had aroused our curiosity. It was a bed of oxalis, or miner's lettuce, a few feet in length on a ledge, with a profusion of brown seed vessels; both the color and the diffusion of light were therefore explained.[105]

When Clyde inspected the duck and discovered fresh grass under it, he realized how recently it had been left. This marker was below the miner's lettuce and thus less than a third of the way to the top of the minaret, evidently on the traversing ledge. From the bed of miner's lettuce, Clyde and Kehrlein followed the intermittent ducks along the slanting ledge and then up a chute. As he went, Clyde became more and more convinced that Starr was responsible for leaving the mystery ducks. Before reaching the top, however, the party was once again chased off by storm and thunder.

The Eichorn-Dawson team returned to the west side to climb Eichorn Minaret. They continued their pattern of investigating as many chutes as possible, and in a gully farther north discovered more rock ducks. Dawson wrote:

> On the 17th, Jules and I went up the second chute north of
> Michael's chimney. [Note: This was the third chute on Michael-
> Eichorn that they either ascended or descended.] We found
> the apparent beginning of the ducks. Some were very wobbly.
> None of them were down. The ducks were usually of three
> stones, although one at the head of the first chute north of
> Michael's chimney was quite large. We saw indistinct footprints
> in one place. These ducks connected with the ones we saw the
> day before. The line of ducks were made by an experienced
> route-finder. Jules and I both admired the excellence of the
> route. We climbed Third Minaret [note: Eichorn Minaret], but
> found no trace of Starr or of his ever having been there.[106]

They descended via yet another chimney, thereby completing their exploration of four west-side chutes and two pinnacles in two days. Once back to the western base of the formation, they returned to camp using a wholly different course that passed over the spur extending down from Michael Minaret to its south:

> Dick Jones and one of the CCC [Civilian Conservation Corps] boys who climbed Ritter (Lilburn Norris) went down to timber in Dike Creek [*note*: a mile or so west of the Minarets], but found no clues. Jules and I went around Michael Minaret over a ridge to a lake. We did so in order to climb up the chimney going down east from the portal, since we could only see the upper part from above.[107]

In this way, Eichorn and Dawson were able to check the opposite side of Michael Minaret, its east face. To get there, they scrambled over the spur and then circled upward to the so-called "amphitheater" formed between Michael and Clyde Minarets. The amphitheater contained a small icy pond. Dawson continued:

> We went down to a lake up another ridge from where we could have climbed Clyde Minaret from the south in a short time and without any great difficulty. We went down a chute [on the east side of the main ridge leading to Clyde], doing a 50-foot rope-down over a huge chockstone (the Minarets are full of chock-stones). [*Note*: A chockstone is a boulder jammed in a chimney that blocks passage.] We met Clyde and Kehrlein searching near Upper Iceberg Lake.[108]

The teams returned to Ediza via Minaret Pass late that afternoon and found that the state police and Civilian Conservation Corps volunteers had given up and left the mountains, having found no clues in the lower elevations around Ediza Lake.

Alone now, the climbers (joined by Starr's friends Whiting Welch and Lowell Hardy) convened a round table. The day's work had yielded more

[87]

evidence that someone had been climbing on Clyde and the Michael/Eichorn Minarets, but there was still no indication that Starr had reached any of their summits. It was confounding. According to Dawson:

> We were stumped. As I write this [letter to Farquhar on August 21], I can't understand it. Lines of ducks lead to near the summit of two major summits of the Minarets, but no signatures on top; Starr usually wrote lengthy accounts in registers I have seen.[109]

Clyde recalled:

> At a round table of the mountaineering parties, after consider-able discussion, it was decided that it would be well to investi-gate the east face of Banner Peak, as there is a dangerous and only once-traveled route up it, which, it was thought, might have enticed the missing man to attempt it.[110]

So, on August 18, five of the mountaineers searched the difficult east face of Banner, the same face that Eichorn and Underhill had first ascended in 1931. No clues were found.

Another conference followed with animated debate, as Clyde remem-bered it. Some of the searchers, including Mr. Starr, Jules Eichorn, and Lowell Harding, concluded that it "seemed inescapable that he fell, either during or after his climb to the top of the highest [Clyde] Minaret, and that he lies on the bergschrund or crevasse between the mountain rock and glacial edge."[111] This deduction followed a logical process of elimination. The crags had been thor-oughly scoured and a bergschrund covered with glacial debris was the only place that could not be checked and ruled out. Given the evidence of recent climbing on Clyde Minaret without any entry by Starr in the register, the Clyde bergschrund was the likeliest site of an accident. Starr must have fallen into the crevasse while making the ascent.

Over Clyde's dissent (he did not accept the bergschrund theory), a con-sensus was reached that any further search would be futile, and that even if

Starr were not in the bergschrund, locating anyone in the maze of chimneys and ribs on the minarets was like trying to find "a needle in a haystack."[112] All agreed, even Clyde, that there was no longer hope of finding Starr alive.

Undoubtedly, Mr. Starr also felt that it was not worth keeping the searchers at risk, and he requested that the group terminate the search. There was now a greater need for Mr. Starr and Allan to be at home. Along with Carmen, they had to find a way to bear the unbearable. They gathered up Peter's remaining gear, and accompanied by the remaining friends and mountaineers, grimly filed out of camp late in the day on August 18.

All the remaining mountaineers, that is, except Norman Clyde.

CHAPTER 9

Clyde Alone

C lyde had no job, family, or home to draw him away from the mountains. The Sierra was where he lived most of the year, so it was natural from him to stay on at Ediza. The basin, once abuzz with state police, forest rangers, Civilian Conservation Corps members, packers, and climbers, fell silent as its population was reduced to one. Clyde enjoyed the solitude. As a student of the Sierra, he considered every morning a new session in his favorite classroom. His daily field diaries recorded his mental impressions of flowers and birds, rocks and hemlocks.

Clyde wrote in *Quest* that he was "not yet ready to abandon the quest . . . [and] . . . declined to accompany the remainder of the party."[113] Even though Clyde understood that there was no longer any hope of finding Starr alive, something compelled him to remain. In his only known comments on the matter, Clyde wrote: "it would afford a good deal of consolation to his parents to know what had happened to him, particularly to be certain that he had not died a lingering death."[114] Those who knew Clyde have said that he was stubborn and opinionated. He doggedly held to the view that the searchers were close to finding Peter Starr and that perseverance would carry the day.

At about this time, a message was relayed to Clyde. A Sierra Club member from Los Angeles named Cliff Youngquist, a man in his mid-forties, sent word to the Forest Service that he had encountered Starr between Ediza Lake and Shadow Lake on August 2. As the rest of the search party departed the mountains through Mammoth, they learned of this news via a telegram on August 18. It read as follows:

On August 2, I talked to Mr. Starr on trail midway between Shadow Lake and Lake Ediza. Starr was equipped with knapsack outfit, and stated that he was going over Minarett Pass [*sic*] that evening and would climb North Minarett [*sic*] following morning.

On afternoon August 3, I found what I believed to be his trail at Outlet Iceberg Lake—Starrs footprints.

Starr left major part of his outfit at Lake Ediza. Convinced you will find his body at foot of North Minarett [*sic*] if portion of his equipment was found at Ediza [a fact reported in the press].

Know him to be such a hearty mountaineer that you will probably find him alive somewhere. In climbing he would have taken the most difficult face of North Minarett [*sic*].

H. C. Youngquist
Department Water and Power, City of L.A.
207 South Broadway
Los Angeles, California.

Sent through City of L. A. private wire to Bishop, then relay through Forest Service office to Mammoth, California.

(Rec. 1:45 P.M., Aug. 18, 1933.)[115]

Because the Forest Service shared the message with him, Dawson had a chance to read the telegram on his way out. He noted in his letter of August 21, 1933 that according to Youngquist, "Starr said he was going to cross Minaret Pass and climb the north Minaret." Minaret Pass was the common name for the steep scree and snow slope between Upper and Lower Iceberg Lakes.[116] Dawson was confused, however, by Youngquist's reference to "North Minaret": "I don't know what that means. The news was sent in to Clyde and I don't know what more we could do except perhaps climb the northern Minaret [meaning the northern-most, now called Waller Minaret] and Leonard Minaret."[117]

That Dawson was perplexed by the use of "North Minaret" as a landmark is understandable. There never has been a minaret named "North Minaret," officially or otherwise. Youngquist was not a climber, and he was likely less familiar with the names of the Minarets than Dawson and his friends.[118] Still, the rest was clear. It seemed that Starr planned to go over Minaret Pass on the evening of August 2, bivouac (i.e., sleep at a make-do camp with minimum gear and no artificial shelter), and then climb an unidentified peak the next morning. The telegram was delivered by messenger to Clyde on the afternoon of August 18.[119]

Mr. Starr wrote on the back of this image: "Looking across Upper Iceberg Lake to Volcanic Peaks from below South Notch." This was the scene in July 1937 when he and Ansel Adams camped in the region. Peter Starr told Cliff Youngquist that he planned to bivouac at Upper Iceberg Lake on the night of August 2, 1933. Ediza Lake is seen at left in the distance. Although lost in the haze, Mono Lake normally is visible on the horizon above Ediza. From the collection of Walter A. Starr, Sr.

Clyde decided to begin all over again and make a systematic search. Ample food had been left behind by the departed climbers, and, with the pressure for immediate action gone, there was plenty of time to be methodical. Clyde himself had already searched two routes on his namesake minaret and had searched around Upper Iceberg Lake. But he had not searched west of the crest. Further, he understood that the Eichorn-Dawson team had not actually been on Leonard Minaret—the pinnacle that was most probably the "North Minaret" of Youngquist's telegram.

Accordingly, Clyde decided to start at Leonard Minaret, just south of the wide U-shaped notch in the middle of the Minarets. (This col is today known as "the Gap" but is referred to in this book as the U-Notch to conform to the writings at the time.[120]) He planned to continue on over the minaret and see the west side for himself:

> Aug. 19th: Went up to ridge north of Iceberg Lake leading westward toward what appeared to be Leonard Minaret, followed ridge westward to base of this Minaret and across a glacier north of it to a wide "U" notch; climbed the Minaret from the notch, but found no evidence; passed through notch and skirted base of Minarets on west side until abreast of Michael's notch through which I passed and returned to camp. Came to conclusion that Walter had not been north of Michael's notch; became somewhat suspicious of the northwest face of Michael Minaret when I examined it with glasses.[121]

Clyde switched from his normal boots to "rubber soles" for the ascent.[122] In the summit register of Leonard Minaret, he left his signature with "Aug. 19–33" (i.e., August 19, 1933) and "up north arete."[123] As he tucked his field glasses away on the summit, Clyde took note of the northwest face of Michael Minaret, now visible for the first time during his search, and remarked to himself, "A capital place for a fall."[124] Clyde returned to the U-Notch, searching for clues he might have missed on his way up. Able now to rule out Leonard Minaret, Clyde dropped to the west base, an entire side of the range he had not yet investigated.

Turning south, Clyde examined every foot of the terrain (on the west side) between the U-Notch and Michael's Notch. He uncovered no footprints. There were no signs of disturbance at the U-Notch. There being only two convenient northerly passages from east to west, Michael's Notch and the U-Notch, Clyde concluded from his findings that Starr had not been north of Michael's Notch on the west side. The results of Clyde's search efforts on August 19, then, were that he could eliminate Leonard Minaret and the region north of Michael's Notch from further consideration.[125]

In further contemplating Youngquist's telegram, Clyde grappled with the meaning of "North Minarett." From Lake Ediza, one must travel south over Minaret Pass, and it made little sense that Starr would have gone *south* to climb a *north* minaret. Clyde apparently interpreted the reference to mean Clyde Minaret, writing that Starr "was also reported as having said that he contemplated bivouacking [before] a proposed ascent of Clyde Minaret." It is somewhat odd, however, that Clyde would have reached this conclusion. Youngquist never mentioned Clyde Minaret, the Highest Minaret, or the First Minaret, as Clyde Minaret was sometimes known. It is very doubtful that Youngquist would have mistaken the name of the most prominent spire in the Minarets.

The following day (August 20), working with the data provided by Youngquist, Clyde re-examined Upper Iceberg Lake and examined Minaret Lake (the next lake below Upper Iceberg to the south) for any evidence of a bivouac. While he had found the handkerchief strip and the faint indentation in the grass at Upper Iceberg Lake earlier, he discovered nothing new at either location. On August 21, he rested in camp. Through a systematic process of elimination, he made the decision to return to Clyde Minaret next. At least two factors focused his attention there: the rock ducks on the slanting ledge (at least one of which had been fresh) and the existence of the bergschrund (where the others believed Starr had fallen).

Many of Norman Clyde's movements on August 22 can be ascertained from his field notebook. While Clyde recorded very little about the search itself or about his detective methods in his field notes, he documented how he saw the Sierra. His appreciation for the mountains and the natural scene around him was obvious as he went about his search:

> Up northeast face of the highest Minaret. Clear, bright morning. Across meadows, around masses of glaciated rock, past deep blue [Lower] Iceberg Lake, with Minarets reflected in its great depths; up scree slope to shimmering Minaret [Upper Iceberg] Lake. Ascend and search bluffs carefully and then proceed to ledge. Climb chute from base to upper end, rock in one portion, steep and somewhat slabby but good; oxalis [miner's lettuce] in seed and some grass in chute but a dearth of Xowers; some loose rock in lower part but very little in higher portion of chimney. Continue from end of chute to top of Minaret. View: Kaweah group far to southwest; Red Slate [Mountain], Red & White [Mountain], Bear Creek Spire, [Mt.] Gabb, Seven Gables to south. White Mountains to southeast across broad valley; dull gray of Mono Lake in sage-clad plains to northeast. Ritter and Banner very impressive to north; Merced group of peaks appearing rather tame to northwest.
>
> A scattering of white cumulus clouds in sky; mass of them moving from northeast and gathering above Ritter and Banner, gradually changing from glowing white to dark blue as their volume increases. Fearing thunderstorms, begin descent.[126]

Clyde's *Sierra Club Bulletin* account summarized his findings for that day:

> Aug. 22d: Ascended to the east base of Highest [Clyde's] Minaret and thoroughly searched about the base of that

Minaret. Followed the line of ducks (found in the previous
search) leading up the northeast face of this Minaret. Found
that they terminated on the arete running northeast from the
summit. Continued to summit and examined cairn carefully
for evidence, but found none. [Note: the register scraps show
Clyde's signature on both August 22 and six days earlier,
with no intervening visits by anyone.] Followed a zigzag
course down the mountain alternating between the northeast
and north faces, using glasses frequently and examining the
glacier bergschrund carefully with them.[127]

Because there was no debris or other sign that would ordinarily accompany a fall off the rock into the bergschrund, Clyde rejected the bergschrund theory of Starr's demise, i.e., that Starr had fallen into the crevasse between the top of the glacier and the mountain itself. The intermittent ducks, however, seemed to chart a viable course to the top of an all-rock route. Clyde's reasoning led him to believe that Starr had reached the summit of Clyde Minaret safely:

Conclusion: Convinced that Walter had climbed to the summit
[of Clyde], in spite of fact no evidence found there; convinced
that he did not fall or otherwise come to grief on the northeast
face of Clyde Minaret, and that there was little reason to think
that an accident had happened to him on the north face; but
if one did that he had fallen into the bergschrund, which was
possible, but not probable. I considered the Highest (Clyde's)
Minaret and Minarets north of Michael's notch eliminated.[128]

Among the remaining possible accident areas were Michael Minaret, its neighbor Eichorn Minaret, and the lesser crags south of them. From Ediza, the shortest approach to Michael and Eichorn Minarets was through Michael's Notch. That was the same route the Michaels had taken in 1923, the same course the Eichorn-Dawson team had followed a few days earlier, and the same way Clyde had returned to camp on August 19. A longer but unestablished approach from Ediza was to remain on the east side of the range, go south over Minaret Pass (the divide between the two Iceberg Lakes), and then continue around to the south side of Upper Iceberg Lake. From there, the route turned west and up a moderate glacier to what is now called South Notch, where it crossed a dip in the Minarets.

Although rarely used in the 1930s, the South Notch route is today "the southerly approach to Michael Minaret."[129] From the South Notch, access is gained to the "amphitheater" formed between Clyde Minaret and Michael Minaret. To reach the west side of Michael Minaret, it is necessary to scramble over an easy spur extending southward from Michael Minaret.

Thinking that Starr may have used this route, Clyde mounted South Notch and explored the amphitheater:

> Aug. 23d: Went around over glacier southeast of Highest
> [Clyde] Minaret, through notch and around to cirque south of
> the Minarets, examining all faces carefully with glasses, seeing
> nothing. On return climbed Minaret immediately southeast of
> notch, then passed through notch and searched about.[130]

The "Minaret immediately southeast of notch" later became known as Kehrlein Minaret, and Clyde's was its first ascent. Having left with the others, Oliver Kehrlein was not present. Atop the minaret, Clyde left a scrap from a brown paper bag that said "Norman Clyde" and "Aug. 23 33."[131]

Through another day's hard work, Clyde was able to cross off Kehrlein Minaret from his list of possibilities, and to determine that the body of Starr was not visible within the amphitheater, thus provisionally ruling out the east face of Michael, the west face of Clyde, and the ridge between them. Clyde returned to camp without visiting the west side of Michael Minaret.

Spent, Clyde chose to rest in camp on August 24. His field notebook notes that it was the "usual beautiful morning and forenoon followed by thunder squall in afternoon." Mulling over the evidence, he "concluded that in the time available, Walter Starr would in all probability have contemplated climbing both the Highest [Clyde's] and Michael Minarets" and that he had "obviously climbed" or tried to climb Clyde Minaret and returned safely "to camp."[132] Norman Clyde, mountain detective extraordinaire, thus deduced that Peter Starr had been safely up and down Clyde Minaret, and that he had next attempted an ascent of Michael Minaret. Puzzlingly, all that remained to be searched was the region already scoured by Dawson and Eichorn.

CHAPTER 10

Dinner with The Farquhars

As Clyde was settling in beneath the hemlocks on the evening of Thursday, August 24, a soiree was commencing at 2728 Union Street in San Francisco—the Farquhar family home. There, Francis Farquhar, forty-five years old and single, and his mother were greeting twenty-seven dinner guests, including Ansel and Virginia Adams, Walter and Daisy Huber, Helen LeConte, and Marjory Bridge, all Sierra Club enthusiasts. Miss Bridge was a particularly special guest. A twenty-nine-year-old photographer, she had met Farquhar on the 1929 Sierra Club outing. Athletic and with a love of the outdoors, she had been one of the group members on a Farquhar-led ascent. Thus acquainted, the couple began a courtship (actively encouraged by Ansel and Virginia Adams) that was in full flower during August of 1933. Francis and Marjory married in 1934 and moved to Berkeley, where, over the coming years, "Their living room was ground zero of the conservation movement in California."[133]

Ominous fascination certainly must have gripped 2728 Union Street that night. The Starr tragedy was front and center. One of the dinner guests was Jules Eichorn, barely off the Minarets, who must have left the others spellbound with his stories of the search. And Farquhar himself had just returned from the aerial reconnaissance.

Farquhar related the Bohemian Club lunch, his water-course search strategy, and his two breathtaking days in the open rear seat of the biplane. He detailed the flights close up to the ancient walls, and the downdraft that caught them and warned them away. But for all his scanning of streams, pools, and snowfields, Farquhar had no sign of Starr to report. Farquhar also was able to describe the puzzlement of Glen Dawson, recently expressed in the latter's letter of August 21. "As I write this I can't understand it," Dawson had penned, "lines of ducks lead to near the summit of two major summits of the Minarets, but no signatures on top; Starr usually wrote lengthy accounts in registers I have seen."[134]

Like a reporter from the scene, Eichorn could elaborate on the discovery of the ducks, the cigarette butt, and the bloodied strip. He wondered aloud why the Kodak, the ice-axe, and the crampons were all left in camp. His narrative revealed the dozens of unanswered questions that remained about the Youngquist telegram, the ducks, the Ritter register entry, the delay of the miners, the unsearched Minarets, Starr's last camp, and other matters.

What kind of person was Peter Starr? What could account for his total disappearance? Most of the guests knew Peter Starr mainly by reputation. Ansel Adams had once looked over some of Starr's mountain photographs, but there remains no evidence that the two were well-acquainted.[135] Although Starr had not participated in the High Trips, the Sierra Club climbers knew of his impressive mountaineering exploits from the summit registers. They also knew that his father had made the grand 1896 exploration from Yosemite to Kings Canyon. Eichorn was aware, based on what he had learned from Mr. Starr, that Peter had been writing a guidebook for the John Muir Trail. Despite the fact that the young Starr had spent dozens and dozens of weekends hiking, climbing, and making notes, Jules Eichorn and Glen Dawson had not met him. Starr valued his solitude, much like Clyde.

The party goers must have deliberated over the conclusion of the searchers and the family that Starr was in a bergschrund, most likely on the large glacier on Clyde Minaret visible from Lake Ediza. Had the snow, ice, and rocks covered him up there? If so, perhaps his remains would be found in another three hundred years when the glacier wasted away to nothing. (Concidentally, the day of the party the *Inyo Register*, a paper published in the shadow of the Sierra, reported that Starr was indeed buried in a glacier.)

Dawson's letter recommended that the practice of climbing solo be discouraged, except, he said, "for Clyde."[136] The pros and cons of that proposition were likely debated that evening. Had Starr had a partner along, that partner could have gone for help. Yet, should even the best climbers be denied the joy of solo climbing and the intimacy with the mountains glorified by the great John Muir and the ever durable Norman Clyde? Would the situation really have been any different had Starr left word where he was headed?

All those at the Farquhar house surely agreed that the Sierra Club itself had done a first-rate and unprecedented job in the searching. The club's robust enterprise had been much more thorough and well-organized than any of the search-and-rescue efforts of the authorities. Self-congratulations were in order. Farquhar already had a broad outline in mind for a story describing the entire affair to be published in the *Sierra Club Bulletin*. Had the tragedy not been so recent, the assemblage probably would have raised their glasses to toast the club's performance.

Farquhar had stayed in constant touch with the Starr family. Mr. Starr and Allan had been valiant in joining the search, but they seemed relieved to be at home, where Mrs. Starr was traumatized with grief. She could not accept the obvious and inevitable. Not only had she and Peter been extremely close, but the situation also was complicated by Clyde's dissent from the judgment of the search party that further effort was hopeless. Clyde's contrarian persistence, no doubt, had left a vague sense of unease.

Six additional days had now passed with no report of progress. The family was not even certain that Clyde was still at Ediza, there being no way to know. Feeling that the time for closure had come, Mr. Starr would announce on August 25 that a memorial service for Peter would be held the following Sunday.[137]

CHAPTER 11

August 25

N orman Clyde had not given up. Rising early at Lake Ediza on
Friday, August 25, he knew nothing of the plans for a Sunday
memorial service. Clyde had a job to do, self-imposed though it
was, and he intended to do it.

By the process of elimination, Clyde had narrowed his search locales to
two areas: Michael and Eichorn Minarets, and more specifically, their west
sides. Their access chutes had yielded the cigarette butt, a line of ducks,
and a few indistinct footprints. The pinnacles had already been searched by
the Eichorn-Dawson team on two successive days. Yet Clyde increasingly
suspected that Starr had been overlooked in that vicinity, unlikely though
it seemed. He decided to inspect the area himself, as he recalled in the June
1934 issue of the *Sierra Club Bulletin*, even finding a new route up the Michael
Minaret in the process:

> Aug. 25th: Left camp early, climbed up through Michael's
> Notch and continued southwest along the west base of Minarets
> to the southwest base of Michael Minaret. Ascended a cliff in
> the west face of the Minaret at first to look around but presently
> concluded that a ledge would probably lead from this shoulder
> into the upper portion of Michael's Chimney, so I continued
> climbing. Found a ledge and followed it around into the chute,
> the floor of which is reached just above a forty-foot drop-off.
> [*Note*: The *Climber's Guide* credits Clyde with being the first to
> find this avenue to Michael's Chimney. This route was further

south than Michael's and the one the Dawson-Eichorn team took.] Continued up to within about two hundred feet of the notch, at head of the chute, and then began to climb the face.[138]

In *Quest*, Clyde wrote that he abandoned the steep, tall, northwest face, because it was too dangerous, saying "This can be climbed but I am not going to do it."[139] Continuing with his earlier entry:

> Abandoned this and continued up [Michael's Chimney] to notch, and from there climbed to top of Minaret. After remaining on summit about half an hour sweeping the other Minarets with glasses began the descent, constantly scanning the northwest face.[140]

So, Clyde searched all the way to the summit in vain, just as had Eichorn and Dawson. It must have been a vexing disappointment. Where the devil could Starr have gone? Maybe the others had been right—it was proving to be like hunting for a needle in a haystack. As he scanned the landscape with binoculars, Clyde must have contemplated abandoning the search at this point, although he never said so. Clyde left his name and the date in the summit register,[141] before another brewing storm over Ritter and Banner forced his descent. He headed back down toward The Portal, probably planning to traverse to Eichorn Minaret. Then:

> As I carefully and deliberately made my way down toward the notch, I scanned and re-scanned the northwestern face. Much of it was concealed by irregularities. Suddenly a fly droned past, then another, and another.
>
> "The quest is nearing an end," I reflected.
>
> Upon reaching "The Portal" I began to follow a ledge running in a northwesterly direction. When I had gone along it but a few yards, turning about, I looked upward and across the chute

to the northwestern face. There, lying on a ledge not more than
fifty yards distant, were the earthly remains of Walter A. Starr,
Jr. He had obviously fallen, perhaps several hundred feet, to
instantaneous death.[142]

It was a historic and poignant meeting of two Sierra legends: Clyde, peering
out from under his campaign hat, rope coiled about his chest, standing among
the ruins of the ancient range as a storm gathered; Starr, clad in khaki with a
white undershirt, arms outstretched, lying on his back on a narrow ledge, facing the heavens.[143]

Viewed from the ground a few hundred feet to the west, Starr's ledge
was situated in the middle of the triangular silhouette of the final pinnacle,
somewhat above the elevation of The Portal and to its right, well below
the steeply slanting ridge line to the summit. Clyde did not check the body,
for that would have meant returning to the near vertical face he had earlier
abandoned—a feat too dangerous to undertake alone. There was little point,
anyway. Starr was obviously dead.

Without delay, Clyde descended, returned to Ediza, hiked to Agnew
Meadows, and drove to Mammoth to wire the news to Mr. Starr that day.[144]

The last photograph in Peter Starr's camera found near Ediza Lake.
The camera was sent to Mammoth Lakes for development of the film. The
image shows Clyde Minaret on the left, the U-Notch on the
right-center, and Ediza in the foreground.

CHAPTER 12

The Highest Monument

Carmen Starr had waited in the big corner house on Hampton Road while her husband and younger son searched for Peter. Extremely distraught, she had been cared for by nearby relatives, who moved in with her temporarily.[145] Mr. Starr and Allan arrived home on Saturday, August 19. Carmen was mortified not only over Peter's complete disappearance, but also by the possibility that he had suffered a lingering and terrible death.

As her first born, Peter had been extremely close to her. He was the bon vivant, the ambassador of the family, the host to all those Stanford fraternity and sorority friends, the lawyer at a successful firm, the child charmed with social grace, intelligence, good looks, and talent. His younger brother Allan, though able in his own way, recognized Peter's special charisma and style, and let his brother claim the limelight. Later Allan would characterize their roles by saying that he had been the son out tinkering in the garage with dirt under his fingernails while his older brother dazzled the family guests.

On Friday, August 25, the family announced that a memorial service would be held the upcoming Sunday at the family home on Hampton Road. Norman Clyde's unexpected news arrived late that Friday. As they prepared for the Sunday service, the family members developed a plan to inter Peter's body where it lay and create a grave among the clouds, closer to the heavens than any other in California. That evening, Mr. Starr wired Clyde instructions: "Do not try to remove remains." A meeting of the two men was set by Mr. Starr for August 30 in Mammoth Lakes.[146]

On Sunday afternoon, two hundred gathered with the Starrs, their automobiles lining the road. The extended family and its closest friends—like the

*Vincent K. Butler, Jr., right, in the Sierra above Pinecrest
in 1930. Photograph courtesy of Lewis H. Butler.*

Chickerings, Stanford fraternity brothers, lawyers from Pillsbury, Madison & Sutro, Sierra Club luminaries, and Piedmont neighbors—flowed into the somber home. As they entered, they were greeted by a giant photographic enlargement of Lake Ediza and the Minarets, the last image in Peter's Kodak, placed over the mantle near the main entrance hall. Peter's ice-axe and crampons flanked the photo, and sage and mountain grass traced the woodwork.

An Episcopalian clergyman called the proceeding to order, then yielded to Vincent Butler, Starr's senior at the law firm. A Rhodes Scholar with an English perspective gained while attending Oxford University, Butler was formal in both appearance and speech. He even sported a bow tie in the wild. During the search for Peter, Butler had written daily letters from San Francisco to his wife (vacationing in Yosemite) chronicling with Victorian gravity the rumors from the field. Although Butler was a tax lawyer, not a courtroom orator, his eulogy that afternoon was memorable.

Facing the assembled family and guests, Butler first quoted at length from an essay about why mountaineers climb written by the president of the Royal Geographical Society. He then recited "The Mountain's Call," a poem that Peter had written only a few days before his death:

God's wilderness is calling me
To shining summits, bright and cool
The mountain trails from snow are free
The flashing trout are in the pool.

All winter long, the lure and spell
Of glittering lakes and towering trees
Of rushing streams and pine tree smell
And flowering meadows haunted me.

Of all the peace on earth there's none
Like evening in my camp fire gleam
No shrine like God's own starlit dome
Nor wine like waters from my stream.

What song like sylvan solitude
Stirred softly by the snow kissed breeze
Or water ouzel's sweet notes tuned
To swirling stream's glad melodies.

Lure of Sierra, wild and free
Jewels deep set in shining skies
Defiant mountains beckon me
To glory and dream in their paradise.

Next, repeating a statement by Francis Farquhar, who could not be present, Butler said:

It is a grand company, those who have not come back. There
are Englishmen—Mummery, of Nanga Parbat, Mallory and
Irvine, of Everest; and the Americans—Allen Carpe and Theodore Koven, of Mount McKinley, Norman Waff, of Robson,
and now, Pete Starr, of the Minarets. The young men of today

know them, and the young men of tomorrow will not forget
them. We all salute them!

A radiant profile of George Mallory, who had died on Everest in 1924,
followed. It was written by one of Mallory's comrades on the Everest expedition. "Mallory's was no common personality . . . But it was the spirit of the
man that made him the great mountaineer." Butler observed that the same
profile could have been written of Peter. He ended by re-quoting the final
verse of Starr's last poem. Sadly, the mountains had beckoned Peter not to
glory but to death.[147]

※　　※　　※

There remained one unfinished duty, left by necessity to the mountaineers. As
Mr. Starr and Jules Eichorn drove together to Mammoth, they reflected on the
fate of Peter. Eichorn surely must have wondered how he had missed the body
during the search. Mr. Starr likely contemplated the details of his son's burial
high on a Minaret, and the family's decision not to retrieve the body. He and
Eichorn discussed the risks of both alternatives.[148]

A day earlier than originally planned, they met Norman Clyde (who had
laid over at Tamarack Lodge)[149] and three others from the east side (Lilburn
Norris, Douglas Robinson, Jr., and Ranger Mace) in Mammoth. On August
29, they all hiked to Lake Ediza and camped in the uplands above it.[150]

The next morning, a "sunny, cloudless day,"[151] they aimed for the serrated
crest. Up and up to Michael's Notch they went, a climb made easier by the low
levels of snow that year, and then dropped over to the steep west side. The
men gathered for a group photograph by Mr. Starr, who had re-loaded Peter's
camera with fresh film. At the base of Michael Minaret, the four youngest
members of the party, led by Eichorn and Clyde, entered the gully in which
the ducks were found-Starr's chute it is now called—and climbed toward The
Portal.[152]

This image was taken by Mr. Starr on August 30 as the burial party left Ediza. The morning light is striking the Minarets. Leonard Minaret is straight ahead.

Mr. Starr took this photograph on August 30, 1933. He inscribed it as follows on the back: "Preparing to make the climb of Michael Minaret to entomb the remains of Walter A. Starr, Jr. Aug. 27, 1933). Eichorn and Clyde made the final rope climb with great difficulty to the ledge where lay the body. They encased the remains in rock on the ledge against the wall. From right to left: Jules Eichorn, Ranger Mace (Forest Service, Sierra Forest), Norman Clyde, Al Norris (CCC Camp lad), Douglas Robinson (son of Chief Ranger Inyo F.)." The August 27 reference by Mr. Starr was mistaken—that was the date of the memorial service; the correct date was August 30.

This was Mr. Starr's first good view of Michael Minaret and its northwest face.
He took this image on August 30.

From The Portal, only Eichorn and Clyde continued laterally across the northwest face. They came to a broad ledge with a perpetual snow patch protruding from shadowed crevices, where Eichorn and Clyde paused to prepare the rope for the final ascent to Peter's ledge. Roped together, they proceeded upward via cracks and slabs. It was dangerous going, but they needed to climb only thirty vertical feet. From the side, either Norris or Robinson took two photographs on the steep northwest face: one of Eichorn and Clyde roping up on the snow ledge and another of their climb toward the body (see pages 116 and 117).[153]

Peter's ledge, a shelf neither as broad nor as safe as the snow ledge, offered Eichorn and Clyde their first close-up view of Starr. Eichorn described the scene to Glen Dawson in a letter dated September 11, 1933: "The body was located about 50 yards west of Michael's [chute] and about 400 feet below the summit of Michael Minaret. . . [it] was in very good condition considering the lapse of time. He evidently had fallen about 200 feet and was killed outright." Starr's skull had been badly fractured. His back and ribs had suffered direct hits.[154] He had fallen a long way and come to rest on his back, arms outstretched. The men found Starr's pocket watch, smashed and stopped at 4:23, on a ledge below the body. No knapsack, hat, canteen, or other personal effects were located—they may still be higher up on Michael Minaret or buried in debris below.[155]

Eichorn and Clyde had carried a large canvas bag with them.[156] When it came time to place Peter's body in it, Eichorn discovered that Clyde was reluctant to help. "Surprisingly, Norman was a pussy cat when it came to dead bodies. He wouldn't touch them. So here I was, a young kid with this dead climber and Norman not wanting to touch it."[157]

Peter Starr's watch photographed by the author. The note on the watch was attached by Mr. Starr and states: "This watch was carried by Walter A. Starr Jr., (Pete) on his climb and fell with him from Michael Minaret. It was found on a ledge below his body. 'W.A.S.'"

Clyde and Eichorn on the snow ledge on the northwest face of Michael Minaret.
This photograph was made during the burial ascent on August 30, 1933. The negative was
not the type made by Mr. Starr's camera and was made by either Norris or Robinson near
The Portal. Mr. Starr wrote on the reverse of the print: "Clyde and Eichorn prepared to
make final climb to Pete's ledge where they entombed his remains in rock."

Jules Eichorn and Norman Clyde climbing up to reach Peter Starr on August 30, 1933.
Eichorn and Clyde are wearing dark clothes. Both are visible just to the right of the center
of the photograph, a rope between them. The negatives for this and the preceding photograph are from the
collection of Walter A. Starr, Sr. The author printed the photographs from those negatives.

Twenty-one-year-old Jules maneuvered the body into the canvas shroud, then moved it a short distance along the shelf to a small cave-like crevice formed by large granite blocks propped against the main cliff.

There Eichorn began the process of entombing the body:

> Near where we found the body I found a vertical crack on the
> side of the mountain that was large enough for the body, which
> was somewhat stiff and not badly damaged because it looked
> like it had landed flat. So I dragged the body over and stood it
> up inside the crack. There were many small rocks around which
> I used to gradually build a protective wall so that the body
> wouldn't slide or anything of that sort. It took me several hours
> to do this, and I finally got it to where it was six or eight feet
> high.[158]

Eichorn then sealed the cave with smaller stones. If Eichorn placed the stones, Clyde, no doubt, helped gather them. Eichorn and Clyde next built a rock burial mound, somewhat smaller than Starr's body, a few feet away to mark the ledge. Eichorn later recounted that Clyde not only refused to touch the body, but that he wept during the burial, having been overcome by the tragedy.[159] Meanwhile, during the long wait Ranger Mace and Mr. Starr watched from below, where the latter took photographs of Michael Minaret from the base (see page 114).

Norman Clyde recalled the rock burial slightly differently. He felt the body could have been lowered (in the canvas bag) and taken out of the mountains, but understood that Mr. Starr did not wish to run the risk of further accident and wanted his son to be interred on the mountain. He noted,

> "So we wrapped him in a canvas. He wasn't broken up much.
> They usually go end over end and crash their head or break
> their neck. His skull was injured somewhat and possibly his
> neck. Otherwise, we didn't see any injuries. We didn't remove
> his clothes. . . . We wrapped him and rocked him in on a ledge.

After the burial party passed through Michael's Notch, Mr. Starr took this photo of Waller Minaret. Ritter is partially visible on the left.

I would have put him a little more to one side. The stones were in the habit of coming down that way. But we put him in close against the wall so that any rocks that came down would go over him [i.e., miss the rock grave]."[160]

Clyde and Eichorn found evidence that very recently a large rock had struck Peter's ledge directly above the body. Looking up the face, they noticed a spot where a large block of granite had pulled loose and fallen, concluding that "a large slab of rock must have broken away as Starr clung to it in climbing, and, hinging outward at the base, had thrown him clear of the face until he struck the ledge several hundred feet below."[161] Thus, the same northwest face that Clyde had tried and abandoned as too risky on his ascent, and that Eichorn and Dawson had rejected on their descent as too dangerous with a storm approaching, had claimed Starr.

In his September letter to Dawson, Eichorn pointed out that the body would have been "very evident" on their very first climb up and that they had missed it somehow:

The first day when we were there searching we must have
been as close as 150 feet from the body. As you will remember,
when we were on the summit of Michael Minaret, we thought
of that face, the N.W., as a possible way down but because of
the weather returned the way we went up. He could not be seen
from the notch but where we first crossed from one chimney
to the other high up Starr's route (the only difficult part up to
where we found the cigarette stub), his body was very evident in
fact I do not see how we missed seeing him on that first trip.[162]

A likely reason that Eichorn and Dawson missed seeing Starr was that in such
difficult terrain they were paying close attention to their handholds, footholds,
and getting up and down safely.

Mr. Starr summarized the mountain burial in an undated letter to Glen
Dawson, probably in late 1933:

Norman found Pete's body where I have marked the white spot
on the photograph—on the left side of the pinnacle about 400
feet below the top. From all the evidence we found when Jules
and I returned with Norman, Pete must have fallen (from near
the top) about 300 feet. Jules thinks a large vertical slab of the
wall, perhaps his hand hold, must have broken off, throwing
him out clear of the wall so that he did not strike until he hit the
ledge, about a foot wide, 300 feet below. Landing on his back
with arms outstretched he was killed instantly, and evidently had
not moved a muscle. There was evidence of a large piece of rock
having struck a narrow ledge somewhat above this wide ledge
which Jules thinks was the slab that broke off. Also his hands
and fingers were absolutely unscratched and this evidence, with
the fact he was thrown out clear, supports Jules' theory of the
slab breaking away and hinging outward from its base.

Mr. Starr wrote on the rear: "Looking west. Banner on right. Ritter on left from above Lake Ediza showing saddle between them and route over east cliff to top of saddle from where ascent to both peaks can be made." That much is straightforward. But Mr. Starr also added: "Aug. 27, 1933 by W. A. Starr." That was the date of the memorial service in Piedmont. However, the processing serial numbers suggest that this was taken during the August 29–30 burial expedition and re-printed a few years later. Mr. Starr evidently confused the date the negative was exposed with the date of the memorial service.

Clyde and Jules were able to entomb him against the wall, on the ledge. That is as it should be. He has become a part of one of the Sierra peaks he loved.[163]

Mr. Starr enclosed a photograph that he took of Michael Minaret, indicating where his son was buried (see page 132). In the photos taken at The Portal of Clyde and Eichorn (see pages 116 and 117), the grave is located above the wide ledge covered with snow. There are few graves in the Sierra wilderness. At 12,000 feet, Peter Starr's monument is the highest in the range, probably the highest in America.[164]

Photograph by Walter A. Starr, Sr., from Volcanic Ridge near the Minarets during the July 1937 photo expedition with Ansel Adams. Clyde Minaret is the prominent peak on the left, Michael's Notch is just to the right of center.
There was less snow in August 1933 than shown here.

CHAPTER 13

Echoes Stilled

There are so few references to Carmen Starr in the published records that one might wonder if she became estranged from the family following the incident. Exactly the opposite was the case. Carmen, known for her devotion to her sons and especially Peter, was strong, articulate, and graceful. Devastated by the passing of her favorite child, she mourned her loss until her own death in 1969.

On September 16, 1933, Mrs. Starr wrote a letter to Norman Clyde expressing appreciation for his resolute persistence and for conveying the information that her son had not suffered a lingering death. "I know of no words adequate in which to express to you the gratitude I feel for your great efforts which finally resulted in your finding our beloved boy." She added: "The knowledge of what had been his actual fate lifted from our hearts a burden that I do not see how we could have lived under."[165] Clyde started a reply but never finished it.[166] In December 1933, Mr. Starr wrote Clyde: "Mrs. Starr is doing very well, she has a brave spirit full of faith—but of course misses her boy terribly. They were very close to each other. I am taking her to the ranch over Xmas where we can be alone."[167]

Mrs. Starr's additions to her ranch book, chronicling life at the Mission Peak Ranch, stopped cold. Before Peter's disappearance, the last entry was dated July 29. It noted that Peter had left "on his vacation to his beloved mountains." Nothing else is recorded until May 9, 1935. On that date, Carmen added the following under the entry for July 29:

August 3rd 1933–
Lux et umbra vicission
Sed semper Amor
May 9th 1935

Roughly translated, this Latin reads "light and darkness come and go but love is forever." Mrs. Starr then left a sequence of pages blank, as if to underscore the enormity of her cruel loss, and began a new chapter. Each year she took care to record her annual pilgrimage with Walter to Yosemite on Peter's birthdate (May 29).

Peter had loved to write poetry and Carmen had loved to read his work. As noted above, at age 12, Peter composed a slate of poems about the ranch, describing the seasons, the natural world, and the comings of dawn and dusk there. He collected them in a thin booklet bearing the date 1915. One poem typifies the rest:

Mission Peak
There stands the mountain Mission Peak
With many a green oak tree,
Where flows the sparkling Mission Creek
While murmuring joyfully.

With many grassy hillocks brown,
And many a wooded vale,
With many a cataract tumbling down,
And many wild flowers frail.

After Peter's death, Carmen engaged the Grabhorn Press in San Francisco to prepare a private printing of *Verses From the Hill Top Tree*, a limited edition of the 1915 poems.[168] The Hill Top Tree was an oak at the ranch in which young Peter had built an elaborate tree house. A photograph tipped into the booklet shows Peter as a boy sitting on a massive limb of that oak. Mrs. Starr's foreword reads:

I see us sitting in the camp fire's glow. From far below comes a coyote's bark. The owls call softly from the trees. The stars leap out. No other place are they so bright. We talk of whether people live on Mars. Now Peter takes his lantern. Out into the dark he goes across the dam beyond the pond. Then up, up against the blackness of the wood the little light goes dancing. The great arms of the oak receive him. Again the little light leaps out and is lost among the stars. And Peter is at home.

In 1914, Peter Starr (all of 11 years old) wrote two short pieces for the piano and played them for the family. They were entitled "Serenade" and "Another Bird." Carmen believed they had opera quality. Accordingly, she had the music properly scored, then adapted two of Peter's poems to fit the notes. After her son's death, Carmen passed on the results to Aurelia Reinhardt, president of Mills College, with the expressed hope that some use might be made of them.[169]

The booklet of verses appears to have been prepared by young Peter Starr in 1915 with the addition of a cover by his mother after his death. The tipped-in photograph shows the two young brothers in the ranch treehouse about 1915.

For the remainder of Carmen Starr's life, Peter was never far from her thoughts. En route to the ranch with her grandchildren, Mrs. Starr would see Mission Peak and burst into recitation of Peter's line of verse, "There stands the mountain Mission Peak." In her final days during the 1960s, nearly comatose, she confused Peter, her grandson, with her own Peter.[170]

❋   ❋   ❋

Mr. Starr channeled his grief into more public memorials. Almost immediately, he took over Peter's guidebook project and made sure that it was completed. He later wrote that the notes were so near a final state of readiness that it was "an easy task" to assemble them into the first edition.[171] *Starr's Guide to the John Muir Trail and the High Sierra Region* was issued in hardback in 1934, printed and bound by Taylor & Taylor in San Francisco, and financed by the Starr family.[172] Vincent Butler, Starr's friend and senior at the law firm, wrote a profile of Starr as an introduction.[173] Mr. Starr inscribed and sent a number of copies of the guide to those who helped during the search for Peter. Glen Dawson still has his first edition copy with the following note from Mr. Starr: "To Glen Dawson with grateful remembrance of your help in a time of need during August 1933."[174]

The most recent edition of *Starr's Guide*, the twelfth, was issued in paperback in 2001. It remains a classic text for every student of the Sierra. When the guidebook, at first privately printed, proved successful, Mr. Starr established a fund with the Sierra Club Foundation to perpetuate future editions.

Peter's notes also were used as the core for *The Climber's Guide to the High Sierra*, first published in 1938 in the *Sierra Club Bulletin*, for which he was duly credited. Since 1954, the guide has been printed as a stand-alone field book. The primary source for the first edition was a mimeographed twenty-nine-page typescript entitled "Comments Upon and Record of Ascents of Major Peaks of the Sierra Nevada by Walter A. Starr, Jr.,—1928–1932."[175] It was assembled from Peter's field notes by his father and Richard Leonard, then chair of the

Sierra Club's Mountain Records Committee.
Through these various publications, a record
of Peter's extensive research and writing has
been preserved, even though his original
notes no longer can be found.

Other recognition of Peter Starr followed. On December 12, 1936, the board
of directors of the Sierra Club approved a
resolution naming a 12,900-foot peak near
Mono Pass "Mt. Starr" in his honor. This
was approved and made official by the
United States Board of Geographic Names
in 1939. Formerly known as Electric Peak,
the mountain was first climbed on July 16,

Walter A. Starr, Sr.

1896, by Walter A. Starr, Sr., and Allen L. Chickering.[176]

As another memorial to Peter, Mr. Starr arranged the private production
of the exquisite 1938 publication of photographs by Ansel Adams called *The
Sierra Nevada and the John Muir Trail.* The book is dedicated to the memory
of Walter A. Starr, Jr. The printer tipped into it the finest reproductions then
possible of a selection of Adams' photographs from the high country. The
plates, made from 175-line screens by the Lakeside Press in Chicago, are
so good that they have often been mistaken for originals. During a visit to
Yosemite in 1938, David Brower was enthusiastically challenged by Adams to
distinguish an original print from a reproduction out of the book.[177]

Peter's death prompted his father to become much more active in the
Sierra Club. By the late 1930s, Mr. Starr, who had long been a life member,
had immersed himself in the organization's efforts. More and more, Francis
Farquhar drew him into the Sierra Club inner circle, and Eichorn and various
Sierra Club luminaries became regular guests at the ranch. In 1940, Mr. Starr
spent a month in Washington calling on senators and members of Congress
to encourage their support for the establishment of Kings Canyon National

Park.[178] Representing the Sierra Club, Mr. Starr gave a copy of the stunning collection of Ansel Adams photographs to Secretary of the Interior, Harold Ickes, who hurried it to President Franklin Roosevelt. Some believe that the book was a decisive factor in the federal reservation of Kings Canyon National Park that year.[179]

Besides overseeing the *Starr's Guide* project, Mr. Starr served as a director of the club from 1937 to 1948, and as its president from 1941 to 1943. Further, he financed, at least in part, the Sierra Club's historic photographic exhibition entitled "This is the American Earth." in 1960. In 1964, after nearly seventy years of membership and service, he received the club's prestigious John Muir Award.[180]

Mr. Starr remained devoted to Norman Clyde. Shortly after Peter's interment, Clyde wrote Farquhar:

> The search for the remains of Walter Starr, Jr., proved a rather strenuous and most puzzling one. I felt, however, that it would afford a good deal of consolation to his parents to know what had happened to him, particularly to be certain that he had not died a lingering death. Mr. Starr bore the matter very philosophically.
>
> He wished to show his appreciation by giving me a check for a rather substantial [Clyde did not finish sentence]. Had I a good income I would not have accepted it, but as matters have been, I thought that it would not be out of order to do so. His approach was a very pleasing contrast to that of one or more others the bodies of whose sons I had gone to a great deal of trouble to find.[181]

Mr. Starr continued sending checks to Clyde. One letter dated December 12, 1957 from Clyde to Mr. Starr, thanked him for a recent check and indicated it would go toward a pair of binoculars and camera equipment.[182]

Mr. Starr was similarly generous to Jules Eichorn. The latter had graduated from high school in 1930, just after the onset of the Great Depression, and had been unable to afford college. He was teaching music to earn a living. Mr. Starr provided Eichorn a scholarship to the University of California at Berkeley, from which he graduated in 1938. A December 1958 note from Mr. Starr to Eichorn enclosed a check with a request that he "invest in some appropriate gifts for your children," and noted that "I am engaged in working on the 7th edition of Peter's guide book—bringing it up to date with the help given by the new U.S.G.S. 15 min. maps."[183]

Generous, warm, gentle, quiet, courteous, bold, decisive, and wise, Walter A. Starr, Sr., lived a long life that enriched many others. He died August 21, 1969.

❋   ❋   ❋

Younger brother Allan Starr, introverted by comparison to Peter, always lived in the shadow of his fallen sibling. He earned a degree in mechanical engineering from the University of California at Berkeley, and during World War II, worked on the Manhattan Project, serving under Ernest Lawrence in the Radiation Lab at Berkeley. An inveterate tinkerer, he applied for and received several patents from the U. S. Patent & Trademarks Office during his life.

Allan lived in Piedmont near his parents (and later at the family ranch), and between 1933 and 1945 had four children with his first wife, two boys and two girls. His first-born son, Walter A. Starr, III, is known as Peter and today resides at the Starr family ranch near Mission Peak. Eddy Starr Ancinas, Allan's younger daughter, provided many of the materials and considerable information used in researching this book. Allan Starr died in 1980.[184]

Ansel Adams and his assistant, Ron Partridge, during a July 1937 photo
expedition to the Minarets with Walter A. Starr, Sr. Adams made the final images for
The Sierra Nevada and the John Muir Trail, *the volume dedicated to the*
memory of Peter Starr. From the collection of Walter A. Starr, Sr.

CHAPTER 14

Fading Light

The last time Jules Eichorn and Glen Dawson climbed together was during the search for Walter A. Starr, Jr. It also seems to have been the last time Clyde, Dawson, and Eichorn were together at all. They did not plan it so, but their paths diverged. Eichorn was unable to participate in the 1934 High Trip, and during 1935 and 1936 Dawson was in Europe, the Soviet Union, and Japan, working and mountaineering abroad.[185]

The very week following Starr's burial, Eichorn continued to push the limits of mountaineering. On Friday, September 1, 1933, he and a group of sixteen other rock climbers motored to Yosemite Valley, pulling into camp beneath the Royal Arches around midnight. The next day, using half-inch hemp rope and crepe-rubber-soled tennis shoes, Eichorn and three companions undertook the first roped climb in Yosemite Valley on Washington Column. It marked the inauguration of an era of vertical climbing that today is still in full flower on Yosemite's walls.[186]

In 1934, Eichorn and Ted Waller, another fabled climber, retrieved from atop Clyde Minaret the note scrawled in blood that Peter Starr had written in 1932.[187] On at least one later occasion (and perhaps twice), Eichorn took Mr. Starr back to where they could see the gravesite and check its condition.[188] On August 2, 1935, for example, Mr. Starr and Eichorn hiked up Iron Mountain (to the south) to get a good view of Michael Minaret (though not its northwest face).[189] Then they traveled north and made their way to Michael Minaret, where they paid their respects. Eichorn checked the tomb to make sure it was not collapsing.[190] Photographs of the range from near The Portal were taken using Starr's camera (see pages 132 and 134).[191]

This photograph of "Peter's Ledge" was made in July 1935 during Mr. Starr's return visit with Jules Eichorn. It was taken from the location indicated in the photograph below.

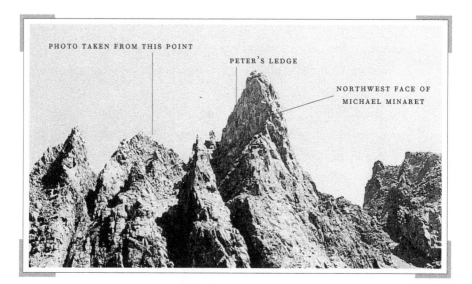

PHOTO TAKEN FROM THIS POINT

PETER'S LEDGE

NORTHWEST FACE OF
MICHAEL MINARET

Using this image from the 1933 burial expedition, Mr. Starr indicated the camera position for the 1935 photograph above. Both photographs from the collection of Walter A. Starr, Sr.

In 1934, Jules Eichorn enrolled at the University of California. Making good use of Mr. Starr's scholarship, he graduated with a degree in music in 1938. Eichorn was hired as Yosemite's first climbing ranger in 1940.[192] For most of his life, however, he was a music teacher in the public school systems, instructing at all levels from grade school to high school. Music and mountaineering were his passions.[193] In 1943, he organized a four-week backcountry expedition for teenage boys to encourage self-reliance. The trips were successful, and he continued the outings for years thereafter, often hiring Norman Clyde to assist.[194]

During his lifetime, Eichorn was credited with thirty-five first ascents in the Sierra, including new routes on previously climbed peaks. Eichorn climbed in Nepal, Alaska, and Africa as well. In 1945, he purchased an acre of land in Redwood City, near Palo Alto, and built his own home. Eichorn lived for some fifty-five years in the secluded cottage with a vaulted ceiling, decorated with mountaineering memorabilia, including prints given him by Ansel Adams in the twenties. Jules Eichorn died in 2000.

Glen Dawson graduated in 1935 from the University of California at Los Angeles, with a major in history. He eventually assumed management, along with his younger brother Muir, of Dawson's Book Shop in Los Angeles, California, the rare book store started by their father, Ernest Dawson. During World War II, Dawson served (along with other climbers like David Brower and Richard Leonard) in the Army's Tenth Mountain Division. During the war, they helped developed lighter-weight climbing gear, including nylon ropes. Dawson says his climbing career ended shortly before 1940, when he married Mary Helen, with whom he lives in retirement in Pasadena today. They are witty, charming, insightful, gracious, and in good health. Dawson has been honored with numerous "mountaineering hall of fame" awards.[195]

Norman Clyde lived on as the incurable mountaineer. Within a few days of interring Peter Starr, he was already summiting peaks in Kings Canyon. He continued to assist with searches and rescues, and in 1934 helped find the bodies of a couple from San Mateo, California, who had fallen together while climbing the East Face of Banner Peak.[196] Also in 1934, Clyde conquered eight of the Devils Crags (in Kings Canyon) in three days. By the end of his life, he had chalked up a total of 117 first ascents in the Sierra (of different peaks, not of different routes up the same mountains). His record stands unmatched today, with no other mountaineer even coming close.

Oddly enough, Clyde himself had been writing a guide to the John Muir Trail, but Stanford University declined to publish it. After *Starr's Guide* was issued in December 1934, Clyde gave up on his project, though the manuscript is still extant.[197] In 1939, he dropped out as the main guide for the climbing parties on the annual Sierra Club outings (after a feud with club leaders), but he participated on the trips in other capacities into the 1940s and 1950s. Well into his seventies, he continued to guide private parties, and wrote magazine articles about alpine exploits. Following his wife's death in 1919, he never remarried or became romantically involved again. Late in life, he occupied the Baker Creek Ranch, a crude cabin in a pretty spot near Big Pine in the Owens Valley. He enjoyed his last high-country camp-out in Fourth Recess above

Photograph from high on Michael Minaret when Mr. Starr and Jules Eichorn returned there in 1935. Mr. Starr wrote the following description: "Mt. Ritter (right) and Ritter S.W. Spur (viewed from near Portal on Michael Minaret)." From the collection of Walter A. Starr, Sr.

Norman Clyde, 1959.
Photograph courtesy of Theodore Waller.

Mono Creek, a little south of the Minarets, in August 1970, at age 85. He died in 1972, and appropriately, his ashes were spread over Norman Clyde Peak (13,956 feet).[198]

Francis Farquhar, who participated directly in the search only by air, deserves credit for quickly organizing the search, and then publishing an account of it in the *Sierra Club Bulletin*. Farquhar eventually wrote numerous articles and books about his beloved mountains, including *The History of the Sierra Nevada*, still the best single volume on the history of the range. He was president of the Sierra Club from 1933 37 and again in the 1940s, and edited the *Sierra Club Bulletin* for twenty-seven years. Francis Farquhar died in 1974. The collection of his papers at the Bancroft Library reveals the thorough and painstaking research of a first-rate historian, the gleanings of a highly-organized and analytical mind, and evidence of a devotion to the public good rarely seen in any generation.

Peter Starr's photograph from the summit of Mt. Ritter looking toward the
southeast glacier July 4, 1932. The main ridge of the Minarets is just out of
view to the left. This view is slightly westward compared to the view captured
by Norman Clyde in his photograph reproduced on page 44.

CHAPTER 15

Exegesis

W hat follows is one possible reconstruction of Starr's final movements based on a critical review of the evidence and on knowledge of the terrain where he disappeared. Its essence is that in August 1933, Peter Starr was attempting a triple first: a new approach to the base of Michael Minaret (via South Notch), a new route to The Portal (now called Starr's route), and once at The Portal, a first ascent up the sheer northwest face of Michael Minaret. While he accomplished two of the three steps, he died attempting the third.

Tradition and lore seem to have accepted a different finale, one that includes a climb of Clyde Minaret. Norman Clyde concluded that Starr had climbed Mt. Ritter and Clyde Minaret (in that order) before attempting Michael Minaret. The Sierra Club placed Starr on Mt. Ritter on July 31 and "perhaps" on Clyde Minaret on August 3, 1933.[199] Other conjecture included an anonymous tribute left at the summit of the highest minaret claiming that Starr was there on August 6.[200] And, the bergschrund theory of Starr's demise, though disproven by Clyde himself, was itself predicated on the belief that Starr had at least attempted to climb Clyde Minaret. A review of all the evidence demonstrates that none of the these suppositions is correct.

※ ※ ※

Can the exact date of Starr's climb of Mt. Ritter be established? Starr plainly and clearly wrote July 30 in the Ritter register, which still exists and is quite legible. But the Sierra Club consistently recorded the date as July 31. For example, the typescript entitled "Comments Upon and Record of Ascents of Major Peaks In The High Sierra Made Between 1928 and 1932 By Walter A. Starr, Jr.," gives a detailed description, taken from the field notes found at Starr's camp, of his 1933 Ritter route. In the typescript, a Sierra Club editor noted the date of the climb as July 31. What could account for this date discrepancy?

Starr's dating system may have misled the Sierra Club. It is almost certain that he scaled Ritter on the July 30, as his summit note testifies, but he probably summarized the event in his field notes dated July 31. The Sierra Club likely mistook the date of his field note entry for the date of the event itself, not having ready access to the summit register that was still atop the peak.

There is corroborating evidence to support this pattern. Starr's summit record on Clyde Minaret (the one written in blood) was dated August 6, 1932. The typescript account of it in *Comments and Record*, however, placed it on August 8. Starr did not return to camp from that climb until 8 P.M. on August 6, and may have waited a day or two to make his field diary entry.

Some might argue that because Starr left the Bay Area after attending the wedding on July 29, and arrived at the trailhead in darkness, he didn't have time to hike in and complete the climb of Mt. Ritter on July 30. But the calendar for 1933 shows that there was a quarter moon that night until about 10:38 P.M., when the moon set in the region. (The Minarets would have blocked any direct moonlight after about 9:00 P.M.) Starr liked hiking at night. "The Muir Pass by starlight," he wrote in 1928, "is one of the most fascinating and weird sights one can imagine."[201] In 1929, he planned an ascent of Mt. Williamson with a return to camp by moonlight.[202] Starr's 143-mile circuit described in Chapter 1 was, in part, made under a full moon.[203]

Furthermore, Peter Starr was used to driving and hiking in tandem, a pattern he had followed time and again in researching his guide book. It would not have been unusual for Starr to have hiked in by starlight on an easy trail he knew well. Or he might have slept by the car or a mile or so down the trail by the river, awakened at daybreak, hiked in, dropped his gear just below

Lake Ediza, and ascended Ritter. Whatever the case, Starr could have climbed and undoubtedly did climb Mt. Ritter on July 30, not July 31.

❋   ❋   ❋

The next key consideration is whether or not Starr attempted Clyde Minaret in 1933, as Norman Clyde concluded. The "blood record," the summit note described in the introduction, bears decisively on this matter. There is simply no Clyde Minaret register entry by Peter Starr dated 1933. A year *before* his death, however, Starr climbed Clyde Minaret and left this account in his field notes:

> Leaving Lake Ediza about 8 A.M. ascended up stream to Lower Iceberg Lake under the pass (following south up left stream in basin). Worked around steep snow bank on left (east) side of lake using crampons and up slope to Upper Iceberg Lake. Continued around right (west) shore to upper end and turned into amphitheater to right. On right side of cirque (3 high points) worked up ledges in red rock into narrow chute. It comes out on ledge (several rough places in it) which runs across face of Minaret. Took second chimney and worked up until further progress impossible. Worked around to right up ledges, ridges and chimneys to point where saw ducks below on ledge coming from glacier route. Worked onto ridge north of summit of this Minaret and thence along ridge to summit. One bad spot short distance from summit where had to drop off of large rock on ridge next to eastern drop-off.[204]

A riveting sentence followed, telling how Starr left a record atop Clyde when he had nothing with which to write (emphasis added):

> *Had no pencil so used blood from ear to inscribe name on film*

carton in box at summit. Returned via ducked ledge to point above glacier. Had difficulty working down ledges and dropping over ledges to the glacier. Worked down to flat part of glacier (with great difficulty as had on basket-ball shoes expecting only rock climb) slipping between ice and rock wall. Continued around peak over glacier (one steep place had to kick out steps) and then around over rocks above Upper Iceberg Lake just under snow field and up a steep crack to a chute leading to the ledge I started out on. Retrieved my knapsack, ice axe and crampons (much needed on that glacier) and returned past Ediza to Shadow Lake at 8 P.M.

This climb is a stiff one and only experienced rock climbers should tackle it.

In July 1929, confronted with another missing register pencil, Starr had left a similar blood record on the top of Black Kaweah.[205] Why would a climber who on at least two occasions had drawn his own blood for ink leave no summit record on Clyde Minaret in 1933?

After Peter's death, Mr. Starr found his son's account of the 1932 ascent, including the reference to the blood record, among his papers at home. He and Eichorn must have wondered how Clyde could have missed such a record in his two summit searches in August 1933. Eichorn went back the next summer to look for it. He reached the summit (with Ted Waller) on August 13, 1934. They found the record loose among the rocks, separate from the register can.[206] Eichorn retrieved it and delivered it in an envelope to Mr. Starr, who eventually presented it to the Sierra Club's Mountain Records Committee. As a result, the first edition of *A Climber's Guide to the High Sierra* published in the *Sierra Club Bulletin* gave Peter Starr credit for this 1932 route.

But in a more fundamental way, the 1932 blood record calls into question Norman Clyde's opinion that Starr scaled Clyde Minaret in 1933, and undermines his reconstruction of Starr's final movements. Significantly, in

Peter Starr's blood record on summit of Black Kaweah
dated July 10, 1929, stating that he ascended from Little
Five Lakes. The 1932 blood record for Clyde Minaret (see
page 13) has a similar scrawl and appearance.
Photograph by Bill Oliver.

supporting his conclusion that Starr climbed the minaret in 1933, Clyde wrote in *Quest*:

> Starr's name was found the following year [1934] by Jules Eichorn on the summit of the Minaret, faintly marked on a piece of cardboard. Starr's diary subsequently proved that the ducks we followed marked his route.[207]

In other words, Clyde argued that the cardboard record, i.e., the blood record, found by Eichorn in 1934 was proof that Starr had been there *in 1933*. The blood record found, however, was dated 1932, not 1933, and Starr's notes document the climb in 1932. There was no record, in any form, of an ascent by Starr in 1933 on Clyde Minaret. Clyde was mistaken, both about what Eichorn actually found loose at the summit and about what was reflected in Starr's diary.

Clyde also relied on three other circumstances, which he set out in *Quest*:

> Almost without doubt Walter Starr had climbed it [Clyde Minaret], or at least had attempted to do so. This was indicated both by the line of ducks on the peak and by the fragment of handkerchief found on the margin of Upper Iceberg Lake. He was also reported as having said that he contemplated bivouacking at this lake the night preceding a proposed ascent of Clyde Minaret.[208]

As for the ducks, they could have been left by Starr in 1932, by the "unsuccessful" party that Clyde had referenced on the route in 1933, by someone else, or by some combination of these possibilities. The fact that a duck, less than a third of the way up the mountain, had fresh grass under it did not mean that all or even any of the others were recently made, for the various ducks could have been constructed at different times. That others were wobbly did not necessarily indicate recency, for a series of ducks, even wobbly ones, may take a year or more to collapse from wind and weather.

The bloodied handkerchief strip with border markings of the type used by Starr placed him, at some time, at Upper Iceberg Lake, which lies at the base of Clyde Minaret. It could have been left from the 1932 climb when Starr cut his ear to make a summit record; he may have discarded the bandage at the lake on his descent. More likely, it was from 1933 when Starr bivouacked at the lake before heading over South Notch. Norman Clyde was probably correct that Starr climbed up to Iceberg Lake and left a bandage in 1933, but it is very unlikely that he climbed Clyde Minaret the same year.

As to Clyde's third point, he was mistaken about the report that Starr contemplated bivouacking at the Upper Iceberg Lake before a proposed ascent "of Clyde Minaret." Rather, Youngquist reported that Starr "stated that he was going over Minaret Pass," the steep scree wall between the two Iceberg Lakes, on the evening of August 2, "and would climb North Minaret following morning."[209] "The North Minaret" was an enigmatic reference that Clyde simply interpreted to mean Clyde Minaret. It is hard to believe that Youngquist, an experienced hiker, would not have known the correct name for the most prominent of the Minarets. Additionally troubling about Clyde's interpretation is that a bivouac was not needed to climb Clyde Minaret.

If Starr had climbed Clyde in 1933, left no record at the top, and returned safely to camp, as suggested by Clyde in *Quest*, it seems likely that Starr would have at least made notes of his route in his diary back at camp, as he had done for his Ritter excursion. Significantly, he did not. His Ritter notes were his last ascent notes from the trip.[210] This lack of documentation suggests that Starr made no intervening ascents between his climb of Mt. Ritter and his attempt on Michael Minaret.

Starr's earlier blood records revealed a mountaineer who was unlikely to climb a peak as prominent as Clyde without leaving a signature. He might even have taken a pencil, knowing that a year earlier there had been none at the register. It was not a matter of leaving records for first ascents only, as Starr had already climbed Ritter, yet he made a new entry there on July 30, 1933. Clyde cited no examples of Starr's having made unrecorded ascents. If he based his statement on the fact that no record could be located for Starr's 1932 visit to Clyde Minaret, the subsequent discovery in 1934 should have cleared the matter up.

In short, it is extremely unlikely that Peter Starr climbed Clyde Minaret in 1933. He scaled Mt. Ritter and Mt. Ritter only. Then, when he attempted Michael Minaret, he fell before reaching the top.[211]

❈　❈　❈

There is more to be learned from the previously-unpublished evidence of four eagle scouts from Stockton, California, who were in the same region as Starr on August 1 and 2, 1933. Their tale bears not only on whether Starr climbed Clyde Minaret on August 2, but also indirectly on Starr's whereabouts on August 2.

Among the summit notes for the Minarets at the Bancroft Library is a paper from Clyde Minaret signed by Norman Clyde and Oliver Kehrlein on August 16, 1933 (and again by Clyde on August 22). The two-hole-punched paper sheet measures about 2.5 by 4.5 inches, and appears to have been torn out of a small, palm-sized notebook. What is most surprising about the paper is the *original* entry—dated August 2, 1933—on the reverse side of Clyde's 1933 notations. It reads:

> Four Eagle Scouts of the Kodiak Patrol—Jack Dozier, 18; Bill Dozier, 18; Thomas Mann, 18; Bob Swenson, 17, made the ascent from the Upper Iceberg Lake while on a knapsack trip on the Muir Trail from Florence Lake to Yosemite. We started up face at left of glacier and soon crossed to chimney on left, continuing to knife edge. All are from Stockton, California's inland port.[212]

This remarkable record indicates that four eagle scouts were climbing the east front of Clyde Minaret and made the summit at the very time that

*Two of the Eagle Scouts from Stockton climbing up Clyde Minaret on August 2,
1933, bathed in morning sunlight with the Clyde glacier to their right.
The two are Tom Mann (above) and Bob Swenson (below). The author
interviewed Mr. Mann and the two Dozier brothers in 1999. Mr. Swenson had
died earlier. The photograph was provided by Jean Mann.*

Starr was in the region. While Clyde noted that an "unsuccessful" party had attempted to reach the summit of Clyde Minaret, these scouts were "successful."[213] Clyde plainly knew of their accomplishment, for he added his own name to their entry on the very same sheet, not once but twice (on August 16 and 22). It is all the more confusing, then, that Clyde wrote in *Quest* that the "front," i.e., the northeast face of the mountain, had not been previously climbed, when he had knowledge to the contrary about the rock route taken by the scouts on the front face of the mountain.[214]

The August 2 entry raises several questions. Did these eagle scouts leave the ducks on Clyde, did they see Starr, and did they talk with him? In 1998, 83-year-old Jack Dozier, one of those scouts, shed light on several of those questions. He reported that the group learned about Starr's disappearance only after their trip was over. Such sensational news caused the boys to go over the details of their mountain journey while they were still fresh in their memories. They had started the day near Rainbow Falls on the Middle Fork of the San Joaquin River, about two miles southwest of Devils Postpile. They came up the Muir Trail, then the Minaret Creek Trail, and camped at a lake close by Clyde Minaret on the night of August 1, arriving about 4:30 P.M., Dozier remembered. (The diary and photos kept by Tom Mann from the trip show that the scouts camped at Upper Iceberg Lake.) They saw no camp fires, no camps, and no one else.[215]

The scouts rose at 6:00 A.M. on the day of their ascent of Clyde Minaret (August 2) and had a cold breakfast. They carried canteens. From the lip of Upper Iceberg Lake, the four headed up over talus and benches toward the base of Clyde Minaret. Their route up Clyde was via the front (east), and was made completely on rock along the summit ridge. Near the top, there was a frightening stretch along a knife edge with a deep gash in it. Without the help of ropes, the scouts worked their way to the top.

Did the boys put up any rock ducks along the way? No, Jack Dozier reported, but they did see a few ducks that were sparsely set. They put up no markers because they were unsure of the route and did not want to mislead anyone who came after them. The ducks that existed petered out about half way up the climb, but the scouts then completed the obvious route to the top. The summit register was a discarded tin can. There was no evidence that Starr had been there, and no register entry for him. The boys descended Clyde Minaret the same way they had come, seeing no one else in the Minarets that day.

After the descent, the scouts did not camp again at the lake, but picked up their gear, dropped to Ediza, then headed down the Shadow Creek Trail and north on the John Muir Trail toward Yosemite. They did not learn about the missing climber until after they came out. From the newspapers accounts, however, it seemed to all of them that Starr must have been killed close by them.

Jack Dozier's brother, Bill, confirmed in 1998 that on August 1 the group left Rainbow Falls (below Devils Postpile), traveled up the John Muir Trail, and detoured to the Minarets. He could not recall the name of the lake where they camped but remembered that Clyde Minaret was visible and that firewood was available that night. He did not recall seeing anyone at the lake or on Clyde Minaret. He remembered ducks between the lake and the base, but none on the mountain itself. The route was fairly obvious, and they left no ducks themselves. Bill Dozier recalled that Tom Mann got stuck for half an hour on a rock face with a knife edge and a twenty-foot drop. The chute they climbed led up to the summit ridge on the north side of the peak. There was no register entry at the top by Starr.

The most significant point is that the scouts did not see Peter Starr on August 2. If Starr had been climbing on Clyde Minaret that day, especially on the route suggested by Clyde, making practically the same ascent, then the scouts almost certainly would have noticed him. They failed to see him, too, when they returned to their camp, hefted their gear, and headed down the Shadow Creek Trail and, without realizing it, past his camp. Because Cliff Youngquist observed Starr that same day wearing his knapsack halfway between Ediza and Shadow Lake, it is likely that Starr was in the elevations below his camp for most of the day of August 2, returning to the site after the scouts departed.

✳   ✳   ✳

What day did Starr die? When during the stretch of days between July 30, when he returned safely from Ritter, and August 7, when he failed to appear at Glacier Lodge, did the accident occur? The anonymous entry in the Clyde Minaret register had him still alive on August 6. The death certificate, old records of the History Committee of the Sierra Club, and Carmen Starr's ranch book all used August 3 as the date of death.[216] A review of the evidence leads to the conclusion that August 3 is, in fact, correct.

First, given the complete absence of any other 1933 summit records in the region bearing his name, the inference can be made that Starr attempted no other climbs besides Ritter, where he left a record, and Michael, where he died before he could make a register entry. That his camp notes covered only his activity on Ritter and no subsequent mountaineering also points to limited climbing. As Youngquist reported, Starr, in all likelihood, chose to bivouac near Minaret Pass on the night of August 2 in order to reduce the time to climb a tough peak, a peak we now know turned out to be Michael Minaret. The next day, therefore, would have been the most probable date of death—August 3.

✳   ✳   ✳

What, then, were the likely steps in Peter Starr's last journey? He spent Thursday night, July 27, at the family ranch near Mission Peak with his parents. Starr hosted and played tennis with his fraternity brother, Whiting Welch, a soon-to-be-married stockbroker from San Francisco, who would become part of the search party. On Friday, July 28, the family left for Whiting's wedding and attendant events near San Francisco. It was the last time son and parents enjoyed each other's company. The final photograph taken of Starr shows him with Whiting, each man dressed in a summer gray suit, hat in hand, with a shoe on the running board of a shiny coupe. Mid-day shadows define their

features, as they prepare to leave
the ranch. Carmen Starr's caption
for the photograph in the ranch
book is "off for the wedding."[217]

After the wedding on the
afternoon of July 29, Starr "left
directly" for his Sierra vacation,
according to Carmen's entry in
the ranch book. Starr traveled
alone by car over the Tioga Road,
then unpaved, through Tuolumne
Meadows, down toward Mono
Lake and Highway 395, then to
Mammoth Lakes and Agnew Meadows. Because Starr was atop Mt.
Ritter the very next day, he must
have driven and hiked aggres-
sively. A strong backpacker, he
may have strolled by starlight for
some distance before stopping.[218] It
was at most a three-hour ramble to
the campsite near Lake Ediza, less
for an athlete like Starr.

*This is the last photograph of Walter A.
Starr, Jr. (right). With him is Whiting
Welch, his friend and fraternity brother at
Stanford University. Welch was at the
Mission Peak Ranch for one last visit
before his wedding. On July 28 1933, they
went to San Mateo for the wedding the
next day. Starr left for the mountains
immediately thereafter.*

That night or the next day,
Starr set up camp a little downstream from Ediza on the north side of Shadow
Creek, a hundred yards or so downstream from the miner's cabin. The miners
first observed his presence, and later his absence. There was little, if any, conversation between Starr and the miners.

Starr's plan was to spend a few days in the Ritter Range, to travel south
along the John Muir Trail, and to come out at Glacier Lodge by August 7,
perhaps re-provisioning there for a further push to Kearsarge Pass. On July

30, he was off for Mt. Ritter, first crossing the sunlit meadow west of Ediza, hopping handily over glacial brooks, rising steeply through the cool of the shade of the hemlock forest stretching toward Ritter, and then breaking out of timberline into full view of his target. Directly ahead, easily less than a mile, was Ritter. The grade to its base was easy. The trees were behind him, and the sun was to his back, bathing the mountain in morning light. The glacial headwaters danced to their own music, and Peter Starr surely felt the exhilaration he had tried to capture in *The Mountain's Call.*

To reach the glacier itself required a short spurt of rock climbing from the base. At the border between rock and ice, he would have attached his crampons and, using his wooden-handled ice axe, begun the ascent. His crampons each had eight metal spikes and were lashed to his shoes with two canvas straps.[219] He used one side of the head of his ice-axe to chop steps in ice or hardened snow, the other, a sharp tip, to jam into the ice and stop himself from sliding if he slipped. He carried a Kodak camera in a leather case with a long strap over his opposite shoulder, and a knapsack. Starr's own description of his climb, found with his camp gear, now follows in full.[220] The account, Starr's last known written words, was dated July 31, 1933:

> On Mt. Ritter lies a large sloping glacier (S.E. glacier) enclosed
> by an amphitheater. The north side of the glacier is bounded
> by the sheer face of Mt. Ritter; the upper-end of the glacier by
> a row of jagged pinnacles on the crest, extending from the back
> or southwest face of Mt. Ritter; the [left or] south side of the
> glacier by a row of pinnacles extending downward from the
> crest. The ascent via this glacier affords one of the most inter-
> esting snow climbs in the Sierra. Proceed from Lake Ediza to
> the base of the cliffs slightly to the left (south) of the lower end
> of the glacier. The ascent of these cliffs is very steep. Work
> your way towards the lowest pinnacles at the left (south) *lower*
> end of the glacier and pass through the gap *above* them onto

the glacier itself. On arriving on the glacier it will be noted that a large hump or ridge of ice, extending from the lower [end] to the upper end of the glacier, separating it from top to bottom into two parts. The part lying between the south side of the glacier and the ice ridge is very narrow. The part [beyond] lying between the ice ridge and the north side of the glacier is very wide and inclines steeply downward as well as upwards toward [that side as well as upwards toward] the upper (west) end. Continue up the south side of the glacier to left of ice ridge towards the amphitheater at the upper end, to a point where a huge crevasse renders further travel upward on the glacier impossible. Some of the pinnacles on the crest above the upper end appear higher than the summit of Mt. Ritter which is above the right (north) side of the glacier. At this point leave the left side of the glacier, climb over the ice and descend across the glacier (very steep and slippery; proceed cautiously making footholds) to the extreme left (northern) edge of the glacier, where a talus slope leads to the summit. I believe the described route to the glacier, via the gap above the lowest pinnacle at its [left] south lower end, to be the most practical route of ascent. I failed in an attempt to scale the glacier from the lower end up the left side of the glacier to this point, due to the solidity and steepness of the ice. The right side of the glacier close to the face of Mt. Ritter presents possibilities of ascent, but the lower portion looks rather steep. Of course, with ice-axes, crampons and ropes any of these routes of ascent are practical.

The weather was clear and the sun blazed on the snow and ice, as depicted in Starr's photographic negatives made that day. Starr, clearly excited by the scenery, used a lot of film during the ascent. All the images are of snow, rock, and ice, but, curiously there are no views from the top of Mt. Ritter, perhaps because he had taken a number of photos there when he visited on July 4, 1932. Perhaps he was simply low on film. At the summit, he made his register entry, stating that the trip up had been "de luxe."

Starr had a commanding vista down the spine of the Minarets. At its far end, he could see well the powerful pinnacles of Clyde and Michael Minarets, especially the latter's steep northwest face and its talus-laden western base. From Ritter's summit, he could have sketched possible routes to the top of Michael. It would have been natural for Starr to think: "I've climbed Clyde. I've climbed Ritter. I will now climb Michael." Such is speculation, to be sure, but the imposing view of Michael and Clyde is not (see the photograph on page 44).[221]

Starr returned to his campsite late in the day. On his descent, he would have had a bird's-eye view of any other campers at Lake Ediza. There he talked with Mrs. Dorothy Willard, the wife of Stephen H. Willard, a Mammoth Lakes photographer. Starr apparently did not make mention of any intention to re-provision at Glacier Lodge, telling her he was planning to go to Kearsarge Pass, an even farther walk to the south. Having driven, hiked, and climbed so far in so few hours, he probably slept in on the morning of July 31 and used the day to prepare the notes about the Ritter ascent.[222]

The evening of July 30 or 31 or August 1, Starr invested his last two negatives in photographs of Ediza and the Minarets, one immediately after the other. Most of the scene is in shade, with the last rays of the evening sun backlighting the pinnacles that are superimposed on a clear sky. They were his last two pictures (see pages 72 and 108). From the perch where he took the images, Starr could see most of his route up Ritter to his right and, to his left, the impending route up to South Notch.

There is no direct evidence about Starr's activities on August 1. There are indications about what he may have done, however. One telling point is that there is no summit record showing Starr atop a peak in the region after July 30. Also, nearby miners noticed Starr's absence beginning on either August 1 or 2, according to the search teams' entries on Mt. Ritter and Mt. Banner. If he had gone down the Minaret Lake Trail, the boy scouts would have seen him. Starr likely spent the day away from his camp in the lower elevations, perhaps on the Muir Trail, probably recording measurements and data for his guidebook.

For August 2, there is both direct and indirect evidence of Starr's doings. The eagle scouts did not see him on Clyde Minaret, nor when they left the region and passed his camp. Cliff Youngquist encountered Starr wearing his knapsack halfway between Lake Ediza and Shadow Lake, a mile or so below his camp, roughly where the John Muir Trail intersects the Shadow Creek Trail. They talked about Starr's plan to go over Minaret Pass that evening and to climb one of the Minarets the next day. Youngquist was the last person to see Starr alive. It was Starr's final conversation.

The most critical point is that Starr told Youngquist that he planned to bivouac that evening above Minaret Pass. Such a bivouac location was exactly on course if Starr intended to make a new, different, southerly approach to Michael Minaret via South Notch. South Notch was the col plainly visible (to the south) from the rock at Lake Ediza where Starr took his last photograph (on the far left). From Ediza, the route would have taken him to Lower Iceberg Lake and then over Minaret Pass to Upper Iceberg Lake. From the far end of the lake (the south end) Starr planned to scramble over ice, rock, and snow up to and over South Notch, the col just south of Clyde Minaret.

This scenario accounts for Youngquist's report that Starr referred to Minaret Pass and used the word "north." It is likely that what Starr communicated to Youngquist was that from Lake Ediza, he planned to go south to Minaret Pass (between the two Iceberg Lakes), bivouac overnight, and ultimately climb a minaret to the "north," or climb the "north" or "northwest" face of Michael Minaret. A camp at Upper Iceberg Lake would have allowed faster acclimation and saved him at least an hour and thirty minutes on his climbing day.

Back at camp late on August 2, Starr likely stored his trail notes,[223] repacked his knapsack for the Michael Minaret ascent, stowed his ice-axe, crampons, and camera, and headed for a bivouac at Upper Iceberg Lake. How did he plan to ascend the glacier without his ice-axe and crampons? He probably felt that the South Notch glacier, with its gentle slope until just near the very top, was climbable by an experienced alpinist without aid. It was a low-snow year, and remembering that he had managed the steep Clyde glacier in 1932 in tennis shoes and without ice-axe or crampons, he was likely confident he could easily negotiate the gentler South Notch glacier.

Starr left his camp in the evening, probably after dinner, once it was evident that the weather would cooperate overnight, and began his uphill hike in the cool of the evening. There was, according to lunar records, plenty of moonlight early that evening. On his way up the steep scree between the two iceberg lakes, Starr must have slipped and cut himself,[224] then used a strip torn from his handkerchief as a bandage or to wipe the blood, discarding the piece of cloth near Upper Iceberg Lake.

That lake, surrounded by talus, offered a logical bivouac site, a knoll of stunted pines about a two-minute walk from the outlet on its northwest corner, near where the bandage was found. Starr was quite a romantic about the high country, and he would have relished a tough night beneath the Minarets. The elements cooperated, however, and the weather that night was good. At a camp near the outlet in the clump of pines on the knoll, he would have slept with the Clyde Minaret soaring above him, eclipsing the western half of the starlit canopy.[225]

On Starr's final morning, he shook off the cold, donned his knapsack, and easily threaded his way through the talus on the steep slope between Clyde Minaret and the lake, moving to its south end. There, he veered up and right over an easy rock ridge, and then met the glacier. The ice and snow, easy at first, even in tennis shoes, would have remained so until near the top. He kicked one step after another into the mantle of frozen snow covering the glacial ice, its consistency softened just enough by the sun to be passable. Finally, he would have arrived at the bergschrund and dropped down into its rocky pathway, following it to the South Notch itself, loose debris and shifting sand being his only impediments. It would have taken him a little more than an hour to reach the col.

South Notch offered a *coup d'oeil*: Upper Iceberg fully spread out far below, with Lower Iceberg and Lake Ediza in evidence even lower (see page 93). Mono Lake and its Negit Island were faint on the horizon, perfectly framed by the intervening ridges, all receiving the slanting morning light. Closer by, the southeast face of Clyde Minaret was terrifying. Across the lake, Volcanic Ridge imposed itself. Down the other side of the col was the dry, easy rock of the Iron Creek drainage.

Once over the crest, Starr easily could have dropped down the short distance into the Iron Creek drainage. At the juncture, he could have taken a detour up to the nearby amphitheater, its inside shaped like a cathedral open to the sky, bounded by vertical walls of Michael Minaret and Clyde Minaret, with a tall entry on its south. At its talus-bound tarn, Starr might have paused for water and contemplated the steep east face of Michael Minaret. Too vertical, he would have concluded, and passed it by.[226] At all events, Starr would have made his way down the sun-baked Iron Creek drainage, and after only half a mile or so, scrambled over and around the south spur of Michael Minaret. Starr had thus engineered a new approach to the spot where Charles and Enid Michael had stood ten years earlier. That was the initial step in his planned "triple first." Perhaps with the Michael's article from the *Sierra Club Bulletin* in hand, he now assessed step two: the challenge of the west side of Michael Minaret. In that article, Charles Michael wrote:

> There is no friendliness about the Minarets. When seen from
> the distance they wear a black and sinister look. Precipitous
> walls rise to the sky-line, where beetling crags cut raggedly
> against the horizon. There are no gentle slopes to beckon one
> to the summit; rather does the scowling sheerness warn one
> off. The spirit of the mountain is the spirit of defiance, and in
> every aspect there is a challenge to the climber.[227]

Starr rejected Michael's Chimney. Instead, he chose a previously unclimbed chimney to The Portal located a little north of the one the Michaels had used, and eventually worked his way up, then laterally to The Portal. In so doing, he avoided the troublesome chockstone described in Michael's article. The first edition of the *Climber's Guide* later pronounced that Starr's chosen route was an excellent one:

> Go up the second chute N. of Michael's Chute to a point
> about 300 feet below the main crest. There cross to right into
> a branch chute leading up the S. side of Eichorn Minaret.
> When near head of chute cross to right into head of Eichorn's
> Chute, thence cross ridge of rock into Michael's Chute, just
> below the two spires. Thence follow Route 1 [another estab-
> lished route] to summit. This seems to be the best mountain-
> eering route to The Portal.[228]

Starr climbed without a rope. For a solo climber, a rope is mainly useful to "rope down" on a descent.[229] Starr eschewed even that precaution. He concentrated on finding adequate foot and hand holds, trying to maintain secure purchase with at least two of his four limbs while searching for the next stable perch, all the while keeping an eye ahead for the best probable route. In confusing or difficult passages, Starr marked his way with rock ducks or cairns, a safety precaution to help him find his way back, and a record of his route, as it turned out, for posterity. At one point, Starr loosed a rock and initiated a slide of debris down the chimney. When he passed from one chimney to the next, Starr paused to rest.

One can imagine the scene. He shed the knapsack, drank from his canteen, and lit a cigarette. It was warm and the day was clear. He was glad now that he had left the axe and crampons and thereby saved the weight—no need for them on the sunny side, just as he had predicted from the top of Mt. Ritter. He was pleased at finding a better way up and avoiding that chockstone, energized by having come so far, so alone.

But the going only got tougher. Above him was the main pinnacle, 300 vertical feet straight up. There were two approaches: one was the way Eichorn, Dawson, and Brem had gone in 1931, up a gully to the ridge,[230] and the other was a harder route, untested, up the northwest face, the face that had appeared so prominently from the summit of Ritter. Starr chose the latter option.[231] He had engineered a new way to The Portal and added a new approach to the base. If he could make the summit via this route, he would achieve his triple first.

Starr's watch, the sun, too, said it was well into the afternoon. He needed to get moving to complete his climb and return before dark. Starr discarded his half-smoked cigarette, shouldered the knapsack, and worked his way laterally to The Portal, directly over Michael's Chimney, then onto the ever-steeper northwest face. With each move upward, the vistas improved: the Yosemite backcountry, the Silver Divide, the glacier-broken jumble of the Minarets, Mt. Ritter and its southwest spur, and Mt. Banner with its signature profile. Starr had little opportunity to appreciate them. The challenge of the rock demanded all his energy and concentration.

Michael had described the difficulty that Starr was facing:

> The final peak is particularly solid and pyramidal in shape, and, like a pyramid, great steps lead to the apex. These steps are very irregular and often missing, a condition which makes progress slow and uncertain. The rock mass is joined in such a manner as to give sloping surface to each step, and the steps are from four to five feet high. The angle of declivity of these sloping steps, or ledges, reached about the last degree of steepness that one could stick to with safety. Often they were smooth and without a single handhold. In order to climb from one to another it was essential to place elbows, arms, and as much of one's body as possible against the surface of the step and then to squirm about until one's knees could be raised to the position necessary to propel the body forward.[232]

Starr was now face-to-face with this danger—and all alone. The northwest face appeared sheer from a distance, but up close, there were a few shelves and ledges, some several feet wide and twenty to thirty feet long. Between them the rock occasionally sloped at a comfortable angle. These enclaves of safety, however, were exceptions chiseled into the vertical.

One such point of refuge stood out. It was a wide shelf with a perpetual triangle of snow protruding from the shadows. It was perhaps one hundred feet from The Portal at about the same elevation. To reach it, Starr would have dropped down a few yards from The Portal and then climbed back up to the ledge. From the ledge, Starr eventually made his way upward on the steeper rock. At some point, to improve his balance, he probably removed his knapsack, intending to retrieve it on the way back.

About halfway up the final pyramid of the northwest face at a difficult and dizzying spot, Starr clung to a rock slab, probably with both hands, either to pull himself up or to maneuver sideways. The slab must have first appeared solid to Starr, a strong but cautious climber. But it gave way at the critical moment. He "pulled" the rock, an ever-present risk that burdens the sleep of every mountaineer. As Starr's slab came loose, it hinged outward, and pushed Starr into space. There was a moment of bewilderment, terror, and struggle. Airborne, man and rock fell together.

Starr landed flat on his side, his head smashing against solid stone. Tumbling down a series of ledges, he came to rest on his back on a narrow ledge, his arms outstretched, facing the sky. The force of the fall crushed his pocket watch and pried it from his pocket. It stopped cold at 4:23 P.M.[233] The rockslide continued its shattering journey downward into Michael's Chimney. The echoes of its clatter slowly faded until only quiet remained.

In 1935, Jules Eichorn and Mr. Starr made the first ascent of a new route up Iron Mountain where Mr. Starr made this photograph of the Ritter Range and he inscribed it as follows: "The Ritter Range (looking north from Iron Mtn.) Ritter, Banner and Southern Minarets on sky-line."

A 1999 photograph by the author from the same position used by Peter Starr in making his last photograph in 1933 (see page 108).

CHAPTER 16

Return to the Minarets

In September 1999, noted mountaineering historian Steve Roper and I shared dinner in Oakland's Montclair Village. Earlier, Steve had commented on drafts of this book. His interest aroused, he had decided to search for Starr's tomb during the previous summer. Along with Walter Vennum, a professor at Sonoma State University, Steve had located the gravesite, and when they returned, he sent me an e-mail summarizing their remarkable story, reproduced here with permission:

> Hi, Bill. Well, with mixed feelings, I paste my trip report here. Was this a good idea? Am I a ghoul? I'd rather consider myself a forensic anthropologist. Let me know when I can return your pics—and I'm sure you'll want to grill me on details. SR.

> On September 17, 1999, Walt Vennum and I set out to climb Michael Minaret, and, as a secondary goal, to locate the gravesite of Walter Starr, Jr. Foul weather hit us around 11:00 A.M. as we reached the Portal via Starr's Chute, and snow flurries discouraged us from going higher, especially as thunder rolled ominously in the distance. So we turned to our next task, keeping an eye on the clouds, which fortunately let loose only intermittently. Thanks to the photos Bill Alsup had loaned me, we were able to instantly recognize the broad, sloping ledge where Clyde and Eichorn had roped up during the burial expedition. This ledge contains a snowpatch for much of the year and makes it easy to recognize from afar, as well as close up.

This ledge is at the exact same level as the bottom of the Portal (a narrow, thirty-foot-high "window" at the top of Michael's Chute—a large chockstone seals the top of the "window").

From the Portal we scrambled down Michael's Chute maybe thirty or forty feet, then climbed unroped (class 3) back up this same distance to reach the sloping ledge. From its right end (looking toward the minaret), we roped up and I climbed straight up (class 4 for a few moves, then easy). I reached a nice belay ledge after thirty to forty feet and saw that I could move around the area unroped with no danger, so I brought Walt up to me so that we could search together. This belay ledge was about twenty feet long, six feet wide, slightly sloping, and covered with rocks and pebbles.

I had noticed, upon my arrival, a suspicious pile of rocks twenty feet from me, on the same ledge, in the direction of the Portal. Although this pile seemed obviously man-made, it looked too small to be the gravesite—maybe only five feet long and eighteen inches wide. And maybe a foot high on average. Furthermore, I remembered that Eichorn had claimed that they had buried Starr in a semi-upright position, in a vertical crevice. I gave the pile a cursory look, lifting a few stones here and there. Nothing.

So I wandered around for about ten minutes, above this belay ledge, searching carefully for clues. I visited the ledge where Alsup had indicated on a picture that an object might be Starr. In fact, this was a squarish rock lying on a ledge, multicolored, about two feet high. I checked four or five ledges in the vicinity, and each and every vertical crevice. Nothing. Back down to Walt's ledge.

At one end of the suspicious pile of rocks, the end facing the Portal, there were several talus blocks lying askew, propped up against the main cliff. Too heavy to move by mere humans, they had obviously been there for eons. These rocks formed a small dark hole, or cave, perhaps two feet deep. I investigated this hole, into which rocks seemed to have been placed. A glaringly white object immediately caught my attention. I hesitated. What to do? I was here to research a story, but did I have a right to disturb the grave? Or was it the grave?

I figured that Mr. Starr would have liked to have the gravesite taken care of, as one would naturally do in a cemetery. If pieces of the body were visible, it might be best to bury them deeper. I withdrew half of a white tennis shoe, smaller than I would have guessed, and excellently preserved, what was left. Walt withdrew a heavier white object from the hole and immediately dropped it, saying, "Sorry, sorry." I gasped, for there was a second tennis shoe with a foot in it!

The ball of the ankle bone (the talus) was a deep amber and protruded upward out of the heavy shoe; the end of the shoe had rotted away, exposing mummified flesh, complete with toenails, half the size they might once have been. We had obviously found the grave and realized at once why the pile of stones was so short: Eichorn and Clyde had inserted the body, feet first, into the little cave.

Now it was time to rebury the objects. This we did respectfully, placing the two shoes deep down into the hole and piling lots of rocks atop them so that not a trace of white could be seen from above. We also scattered some of the pile of rocks, and the "suspicious" pile of rocks is now much more natural looking and certainly doesn't look like a gravesite. I think this was a good idea, although perhaps we should have left it as is.

A few mysteries remain. Where are the bones? While I didn't really uproot rocks from the main pile, I did enough investigating to see that the bedrock of the ledge was often visible beneath the pile. I did this for the entire five feet of the pile. Not a trace of any bones, though obviously ribs and leg bones and skull should have been there.

A second mystery: why did Eichorn claim to have buried the body semi-upright? This ledge is absolutely flat. His interview, as I recall, was done many years later and I assume his memory failed him.

Yet another mystery: a really long fall is out of the question, and why this was assumed till now is odd. I carefully checked out the terrain above the gravesite. Because of the hugely sloping nature of the ridge that falls off northwest from the summit, Starr couldn't have fallen more than 125 feet if he landed on the ledge where he is buried—he would have reached the ridge after this distance and immediately moved off left toward the summit. Moreover, the reports of him being "in surprisingly good shape" might be viewed with some skepticism.

The cliffs above my high point, however, are in fact pretty steep—serious climbing would be involved. But, falling from this area, he would have smashed into many ledges before landing on his ultimate one. It's inconceivable to me that he would be in good condition. Eichorn could have told Mr. Starr this to comfort him, and he could have told Dawson the same story so as not to have the truth come out. Or, somehow more likely to me, if the body was truly in good condition, then he may not have fallen far at all. Is it possible that he simply slipped (with tennis shoes!) a few feet above the gravesite and was knocked unconscious and never woke up—or lay there for a few days, paralyzed, and then died? We'll never know.

Three other matters: the evidence of rockfall seen by Eichorn was probably insignificant since any rock that Starr might have pulled off would have fallen directly down into the dark, dank depths of Michael's Chute (the way we came down). Eichorn would not have been able to see this particular rockfall evidence because they went up a totally different way.

Second, the mystery of the pack. The pack, had it fallen off Starr, would also have landed directly into Michael's Chute, near the upper chockstone. Hundreds of people have been in his hideous place, including Clyde on the 25th, when he circled around "Clyde's ledge" and into Michael's Chute. It would be impossible to miss a pack, as the chute is but fifteen feet wide in most places.

Third, the time of death. It took us four hours to get back to Ediza from the gravesite. We moved like slugs, true, and Starr was a young tiger. But I still wonder why anyone would be high on the minaret after 4:30. Doesn't make sense. I'd say the watch simply stopped that morning because he forgot to wind it during his cold bivouac.[234]

Our dinner first involved swapping stories about the Deep South and the sixties. Among his many other accomplishments, Steve was a volunteer in the second protest march over the Pettus Budge in Selma, Alabama, in 1965. Those stories alone could have fully occupied our conversation. But I was anxious to learn about Starr. I pulled out photographs from 1933 and 1935 that I had shared with Steve before his climb. He was familiar with the two prints showing Eichorn and Clyde roping up and climbing above the snow ledge. He pointed to a white fuzzy speck that he felt must have been Peter's body, right atop the apex of the huge boulder up from and to the right of the snow patch. That apex was on the ledge where Roper found Starr's remains. There is, indeed, a fuzzy white speck in both photographs that could well have been Starr's white undershirt, with Starr stretched out horizontally. It is hard to tell for sure.

Steve described his climb again, The Portal, the snow ledge, Peter's Ledge, the talus cave, the pile of man-made rocks adjacent to it. The image formed in my mind of Starr having been buried in a makeshift way with both his feet and legs tucked into the talus cave (a chamber too short for his entire body) with his torso and head under a man-made rock pile adjacent to the cave. But what would account for the absence of all his bones except the one foot and ankle? Had climbers cannibalized the grave? No way, we concluded, for Steve would have heard of such activities. His ear has long been to the ground of Sierra lore. Had it been the ravishes of time in harsh terrain, we wondered? Perhaps the ankle had been protected from small animals by the tennis shoe. Steve noted that Eichorn's much-later description of placing Peter in a vertical position was obviously inaccurate.

As we talked, I felt increasing admiration for Steve. Hardly a week earlier he had been high on Michael Minaret breathing the air and handling the rock that Norman Clyde, Jules Eichorn, Glen Dawson, and Peter Starr had breathed and handled, as if time had been arrested. Had it been the right thing to do, we asked, to go up and disturb the grave? Presumptuously, I expressed my opinion that Starr's parents and Peter himself would have wanted it so and would have been grateful that the current generation of mountaineers had paid its respects and tended to the grave.

Would it be right, we also asked, to publish the gravesite's whereabouts? Climbers, we agreed, have integrity. Anyone capable enough to reach the base of Michael Minaret, and particularly to reach Peter's Ledge, would do so, almost by definition, with honorable intentions. Its location should be recorded so that the best and ablest of Peter's successors can, as did Steve and Walt, honor the memory of this fallen hero.

※　　※　　※

My son, John, then 11, and I sat on the rock outcrop near the cascade where we imagined that Peter Starr had paused to sip on his last visit to Mt. Ritter.

On our left, we heard the cascade roaring from behind us and running down and down to Ediza, sparkling blue within an oval of bright green. The whole 1933 stage was spread about us. The Minarets raced upward on our right. Ritter loomed behind us. Volcanic Ridge and Minaret Pass imposed themselves a mile away, dead ahead. At timberline, we gazed over the sea of ancient mountain hemlocks. The afternoon light was pleasant. This camp was our reward for a tough cross-country hike via the ridge from Garnet Lake on a day that started farther north.

Enjoying the moment, my focus drifted in time. In the meadows up from Ediza, near another stream flowing down from the Minarets, I imagined a group of twenty, broken into smaller conferences, pointing about in earnest. I explained to John that in the 1930s, an expert climber, out all alone, was trying to reach the top of a minaret and fell and died. No one knew that it had happened. When he did not return, a search party came looking. The climber's father was in the search party. So were some famous climbers. Their base camp was right down there, I pointed, in the uplands among the hemlocks. There was even an airplane hunting, too, for the first time in the Sierra. The missing man was up so high, hidden among the rocks, that no one could find him.

After several days, I continued, everyone gave up and went home—except one stubborn fellow, the best mountaineer in the history of the range, who stayed on and kept looking. Day after day, he looked, all alone, making some dangerous ascents along the way. Finally, he found the lost climber and buried him in a rock grave high on the mountain. The body is still there. His grave is the highest in the Sierra, and probably in all of the United States. The lost climber left behind a book about the Sierra. Thousands still read it every year. When you are older, you will have read and re-read it too. For a moment, in the casual way of the living, we both stared at the Minarets.

Afterword: A Comment on the Investigation

My original goal was to write a book about the area in the Sierra Nevada that included Lake Ediza and the Ritter Range, one of my favorite backpacking venues. I had long known of the Starr incident in its broadest outline and felt it would make up one chapter in a larger volume. But the story captured my fascination and soon monopolized my endeavor.

In 1998, Jim Snyder, historian for the National Park Service in Yosemite, put me in touch with Glen Dawson, then 87 years old and in good health. Glen and Mary Helen, his wife, had just moved into a sunny apartment in Pasadena and were going through old files and tossing many out. He said he had almost thrown out the package he soon sent me on Starr. A correspondence developed. My mailbox was treated to additional artifacts from time to time. I visited Glen and Mary Helen in January 1999. It was one of the high points of this project. What wonderful lives they have led.

Steve Roper, another Sierra legend, gave me Jules Eichorn's address and, after an introductory phone call, my assistant Kathy Young and I visited Jules and Shirley Eichorn in Redwood City. Jules' memory was not so good, at least with strangers like me. Shirley provided some materials, however, the most interesting of which was a set of cassette tapes of an interview, never before published, that Jules gave in about 1990 to Robert Lyhne, a journalist. The interview provides new information on the Starr search and is quoted in the book. Kathy transcribed the relevant parts of the tapes. In fact, Kathy typed many drafts of the manuscript for this book, fielded many return calls and became a regular acquaintance with Glen, Shirley, and many others. She read and proofed page after page and was indispensable to this project, even proposing the title that was chosen for the book. A friend of Jules, another hero from the golden era of Sierra climbing, Ted Waller, was good enough to read a draft of this book and provide insights. Ted now lives in Oregon. Peter Farquhar, the son of Francis Farquhar, met with me and provided relevant excerpts from his father's calendar/diary, which formed the basis for the chapter on the Farquhar dinner party.

I had used the Bancroft Library at the University of California at Berkeley when I performed research for my prior book *Such A Landscape!* (about the 1864 Brewer expedition in the Sierra); I am also a member of the Friends of the Bancroft Library. Sierra mountain registers and Sierra Club members' papers are there, as are some of Norman Clyde's papers. As early as 1958, the Sierra Club initiated discussions with the Bancroft Library to archive the extensive collection of Sierra summit records amassed by the club in San Francisco. The discovery of the 1932 blood record, described in the introduction, and learning of the eagle scouts, detailed in Chapter 15, were two exciting moments for me at the Bancroft. David Farrell, Ann Lage, and James Eason of the Bancroft Library went beyond the call of duty to assist this project.

Somewhat less helpful these days is the Sierra Club Library. The library has a complete collection of the *Sierra Club Bulletin* and old maps, but otherwise is a mere shadow of its former self. The part-time Sierra Club librarian, Ellen Byrne, was an enthusiastic asset, however, and stretched her hours more than once to help. Fortunately, much of the Sierra Club's historical materials are in the Bancroft Library. Another library that helped me was the Eastern California Museum in Independence, California, sending me the 1972 *Climbing* article with the last published interview of Norman Clyde.

After I found the eagle scouts' August 2 entry, I wondered whether any of the group was alive and might still recall that day in 1933. Using a "people finder" and the Internet, I was surprised at how quickly I was talking to three of them by phone. In a whiz, the ancient artifact came to life! "Captain Jack" Dozier and his brother Bill still lived (in 1998) in Stockton. Tom Mann lived in

Orinda. Bob Swensen was dead. I interviewed the three survivors. Later, after Tom Mann died, his son found Tom's diary and photos, and sent them to me.

In reading the old newspaper accounts, I was thrilled to learn that the Starr family residence had been at 216 Hampton Road in Piedmont, only four blocks from my own home. My jogging route had gone right by the Starr house for twenty-five years. I left my card in the mailbox, and my wife Suzan and I later were rewarded with a tour of this lovely Julia Morgan on a shaded corner lot, and an introduction to the descendents of the Starr family. The present occupants, Don and Stephanie Mooers, acquired the home directly from the estate of the Starrs, and are only its second owners.

Unmarried, Peter Starr left no children. Allan, his brother, had four, who are all quite well. Eddy Ancinas, a writer who lives in Lake Tahoe and San Francisco, loaned me Carmen's ranch books, family scrapbooks, Starr's 1926 27 correspondence, and other memorabilia—even the original of *Verses From the Hill Top Tree* by young Peter Starr at age 12. Eddy also furnished me what she thought was Starr's ice-axe and watch to photograph. The watch was indeed Peter Starr's (see page 115), but the ice-axe is apparently that of Mr. Starr, Sr. It is identical to Peter's Swiss-made axe, which was first loaned to the Sierra Club's Le Conte Memorial in Yosemite Valley, and wound up eventually with Peter's crampons at the Oakland Museum. At last check, they were still on display in its California history section (under Accession Nos. H84.328.1 and H84.328.6).

Walter A. Starr, III, also known as Peter, now lives at the Starr family ranch near Mission Peak. He, too, was cooperative and allowed me to rummage through his ranch-house basement, through old grocery boxes that had once been in the barn and had begun to be meals for rodents. There I found a lot of negatives and prints tossed randomly in the boxes; the most interesting of the lot was a processed film envelope marked in pencil by Mr. Starr: "Pete's last Ritter film." I am an amateur photographer and, with the family's permission, made a set of prints from this set. Other envelopes, on close study, revealed Mr. Starr's negatives (and prints) from the burial expedition, as well as from the 1935 and 1937 return visits. Selected images taken by both Peter and Mr. Starr are reproduced in this book.

At least five items were missing or misplaced from the Norman Clyde Collection at the Bancroft Library. The most regrettable loss, from the perspective of this project, was the missing Cliff Youngquist telegram to Norman Clyde dated August 18, 1933; it provided information on Youngquist's conversation with Starr at Ediza Lake. The inventory showed it was once in the collection. The Norman Clyde Collection was made possible, in the first place, by two Clyde scholars, David Bohn and Mary Millman of Berkeley, who acquired a large body of his papers and photographs near the end of Clyde's life. David Bohn was responsible for *Norman Clyde Of The Sierra Nevada*. Mary Millman reviewed much of the collection, archived four boxes of it, then gave it to the Bancroft, where it is referred to as the Norman Clyde Collection B. L. 79/33C. David and Mary were quite helpful in my project and agreed to try to find copies of the missing evidence. Mary Millman scoured her own private collection and found replacement copies. (She later went to the Bancroft and found most of the missing items, misfiled.) What a miracle worker!

Steve Roper, Bill Oliver, Jim Snyder, Bob Eckart, Paul Gallez, and Steve Medley, all far better mountaineers than myself, read drafts and provided superb insights and information. I was honored to interview David Brower, Morgan Harris, Ted Waller, and Ron Partridge along the way. My hiking friends Jim Garrett and Joe Garrett not only read drafts but encouraged me in every way to finish this work. My son John was with me on three important trips to the Minarets. On one we climbed to South Notch, found Peter's last camp below Lake Ediza, and sat where Peter had sat to take his last photograph. With us on that excursion were Sidney Craft, Joe Turnage, Joan and Marc Reiss, Walter Dowdle, and Doug Kern. My son, John, has accompanied me on many Sierra outings. (Now, it seems, I accompany him.)

Many dry holes, of course, were drilled in this project. Checks at the ranger stations at Mammoth Lakes and Bishop turned up nothing, not even a summary report. Pillsbury, Madison & Sutro, Peter Starr's law firm, could supply no details about Peter Starr after all these years. The coroner for Madera County (the Minarets are in Madera County) could supply only a death certificate and no report. Lilburn Norris and Douglas Robinson, Jr., two youngsters when they joined the search party and burial expedition, have sunk without a trace. (The Douglas Robinson, Jr., who writes about mountaineering is no relation.) Inquiries of Delta Kappa Epsilon, Stanford University Library, the Federal Records Center, and the University of California at Los Angeles Library came back negative. There were many more research avenues that were explored.

As I unearthed evidence, I had to evaluate its probative value, exercise some judgment, and then try to reconstruct the story, somewhat like an archeologist recreating a civilization from shards of ancient pottery. Most reliable were contemporaneous accounts and photographs (except for the newspaper stories, which were usually only about half-correct in their details). I drew on my twenty-five years as a trial lawyer in sizing up evidence, as well as my quarter-century of hiking and climbing in the Sierra. In this book I have tried, however, to provide enough of the actual record so that readers can make their own judgments, for, without question, the evidence is sometimes subject to multiple interpretations.

Two ongoing mysteries loom large. First, Peter Starr's field notes/maps and his draft manuscript for *Starr's Guide* and *Comments and Record* could not be located. One would have thought that Mr. Starr, given his devotion to Peter, would have donated his and Peter's papers to the Bancroft Library. Ann Lage of the Bancroft Library was diligent in searching for them and confirmed to me that they are simply *not* at the Bancroft. Alternatively, one would think that they might have been given to the Sierra Club, but evidently not; they were not donated to the California Historical Society (in which Mr. Starr was active), nor to the Society of California Pioneers, nor to Stanford University, nor to Sierra Club Books (the recipient of the Starr family grant for perpetual publication of the field book). No member of the family has them, and they probably were thrown out when the Hampton Road house was sold upon Walter and Carmen's deaths. Even the attic at 216 Hampton Road was checked with no luck. How much I wanted (and still want) to see them, and how hard I dug to find them. Fortunately, a large part of their contents was reproduced in the first edition of *Starr's Guide* and in *Comments and Record*. Starr's personal notes diary will, it seems, be lost to history. (A related loss is that of Mr. Starr's own diary from the time he spent in Alaska. I like to imagine that Mr. Starr put both diaries somewhere for safekeeping and that this treasure trove will reveal itself in time.)

Second, Starr's canteen and knapsack (and any notes within it) were never recovered from Michael Minaret. Eichorn's letter to Dawson indicated that the burial party found no personal effects other than Starr's watch on Michael Minaret. I suspect that the knapsack contained notes regarding Starr's activities. I further surmise that Starr, as he had done on Clyde Minaret a year before, removed his knapsack, perhaps in order to improve his balance— with the idea that he would retrieve it on his return. It was not necessary for Eichorn and Clyde to climb any higher than the body, so they made no searches for such items among the ledges higher up the face. Steve Roper went a few feet above the body in 1999, but not much higher, not up to the area from which Peter likely fell. Given what the ravishes of time did to the body itself, it is highly unlikely that a canvas knapsack has weathered two-thirds of a century. Peter Starr proved how dangerous was the climb; readers definitely should not repeat the act.

Afterword to the 2010 Edition

Since *Missing in the Minarets* was first published a decade ago, I have heard from many of its friends. Here are the updates that will be of most interest to readers.

Missing (at page 126) had a small role in renewing interest in the 1938 Ansel Adams publication *Sierra Nevada: The John Muir Trail*. In 2006, an exquisite reissue of the book was painstakingly produced by the Ansel Adams Publishing Rights Trust, with a gracious reference to *Missing* in the new foreword. While this reissue was in process, we learned that the last negative taken by Pete at Lake Ediza, which I had been unable to find, was among Ansel Adams' negatives at the Center for Creative Photography at the University of Arizona. Pete's father had left it with Adams for safekeeping. A number of prints had been made in 1933 from the negative, and one of those prints was used for the image on page 108.

Eddy Ancinas and other Starr family members have now donated to the Bancroft Library a wealth of photographs, letters, and notes from Pete and his father. These were of tremendous assistance in writing *Missing*. I have likewise donated to the Bancroft all of the research materials I have collected from various sources.

Thanks to Michael Rettie of Alameda, a treasure trove of negatives from Sierra Club High Trips has been saved from the dumpster, including several of the Glen Dawson negatives published in *Missing* (pages 46, 51, 57, 59, 60, 63, and 65). These were purchased en masse by Michael for five dollars at an estate sale in the 1990s. After reading *Missing*, he eventually figured out the negatives were from the collection of Lewis Clark, a Sierra Club official in the

1930s. Michael has scanned many of the negatives and they are now viewable at www.thehighsierra.org.

Pete Starr's former law firm provided me with a reminiscence of Pete by Francis Marshall, an attorney who had practiced with him. He said, among other things, "[Pete] was a truly sweet person, unfailingly courteous and rather shy, a confirmed bachelor." The firm's "Time Book and Pay Roll" ledger for July 1933 shows Pete's last day at work was July 28 (he worked seven and a half hours), and the 29th is shown as a vacation day (consistent with the text on page 15 of this book).

Among several items that came from Harv Galic is a copy of the *Los Angeles Times* from June 20, 1915 (page iii6), which carried an announcement of the wedding of Miss Winifred M. Bolster to Professor Norman A. Clyde at her home at 88 West Mountain Street. For more on the Rettenbachers (page 209, note 196), see Harv Galic, "Lonely Grave in the Sierra," www.stanford. edu/~galic/rettenbacher. By way of correction, it was Allie W. Robinson, an Inyo-Mono packer and friend of Clyde, not Chief Ranger Douglas Robinson, who sent the note to Clyde to come aid in the search for Starr (page 50); otherwise, *Missing* correctly portrays Ranger Robinson's role in the search. Contrary to *Missing* (page 54), the first aerial search in the Sierra Nevada was not the search for Starr; the *Los Angeles Times* reported on July 17, 1930 (page A1), that army airplanes were then being used to look for a lost boy near Mount Whitney.

Glen Dawson is still very much alive in Pasadena. God bless him. I wish that my good friend Steve Medley, the beloved president of the Yosemite Association, had lived to see the full success of *Missing*. A gifted writer and editor, Steve guided the original manuscript through its most critical stages of organization and design, as he did for so many Sierra publications. A 2006 tragedy along the Merced River ended Steve's brilliant trace across the Yosemite sky.

William Alsup
Oakland, July 2010

Endnotes

Frequently repeated citations are abbreviated as follows:

B. L.: Bancroft Library.

Climber's Guide: Steve Roper, *The Climber's Guide to the High Sierra* (San Francisco: Sierra Club Books, 1976).

Climbing: Tom Miller, "First on the Most." *Climbing* (May–June 1972): 3–6.

Comments and Record: "Comments Upon And Record of Ascents of Major Peaks In the High Sierra Made Between 1928 and 1932 by Walter A. Starr, Jr." (1934). Several copies are scattered throughout the Bancroft Library at the University of California at Berkeley. One is in the Francis Farquhar Collection at C-B 517, CTN 4. Another is held in the Sierra Club Mountain Register and Records Collection at 71/293 C, CTN 2, Folder 24.

Dawson-Farquhar 8/21/33 Letter: Glen Dawson's letter to Francis Farquhar dated August 21, 1933, reporting on the search.

Eichorn-Lyhne Interview: In about 1990, Jules Eichorn was interviewed on audio tape by Robert Lyhne, a journalist and friend of the Eichorn family. The interview was never published. The eight cassettes of this interview were made available to the author by Shirley Eichorn, Jules' wife. A partial transcript was made of the relevant passages by Kathy Young.

Mountain Records: Mountain Records of the Sierra Nevada, a mimeographed booklet compiled by Richard Leonard (on behalf of the Sierra Club's Committee on Mountain Records) in 1937. A copy of it is in the Bancroft Library in the Francis Farquhar Papers at c-b 517, ctn 4.

NCSN: Norman Clyde, *Norman Clyde of the Sierra Nevada: Rambles through the Range of Light* (San Francisco: Scrimshaw Press, 1971).

Quest: The chapter entitled "The Quest For Walter Starr" in Norman Clyde, *Norman Clyde of the Sierra Nevada: Rambles through the Range of Light* (San Francisco: Scrimshaw Press, 1971).

SCB (June 1934): "The Search for Walter A. Starr, Jr." *Sierra Club Bulletin* 19, no. 3 (June 1934): 81 85.

Starr's Guide: Walter A. Starr, Jr., *Starr's Guide to The John Muir Trail and the High Sierra Region*. A copy of the first (1934) edition, published within the *Sierra Club Bulletin*, is in the Bancroft at F868.s5s85. Twelve editions have been published. Some citations (as indicated) are to the eleventh edition (San Francisco: Sierra Club Books, 1974).

For consistency, the following spellings and usages appear throughout, even in quotations, regardless of the usage of the original author: Michael Minaret, Michael's Notch, and Michael's Chimney.

CHAPTER I

1.   For a history of the development of the John Muir Trail, see Walter Huber, "The John Muir Trail," *Sierra Club Bulletin* 15 (1930): 37; LeConte, "The High Mountain Route Between Yosemite and the King's River Canyon," *Sierra Club Bulletin* 12 (1909): 1.

2.   Sources for this paragraph are *SCB (June 1934)*, 49; *Starr's Guide* (11th ed.), ix-xi; *Comments and Record*, passim; and Starr Family Ranch Book (1930 1940), made available to author by Ms. Eddy Ancinas. The source for Starr's climbing

"without rope" is page 1 of *Comments and Records*: "He never used a rope in climbing and was usually alone."

3.   On January 8, 1927 in Milan, Starr wrote his parents: "In France everyone seems to expect another war within ten years. There is a great deal of talk of a war with Italy, but this seems impossible as Italy would not stand a chance. However, Italy has been concocting a treaty with Germany with whom she has always been friendly. The main reason she joined the Allies in the Great War was her hostility to Austria. Germany owned a great deal of Italy before the war." The letter was made available to the author by Walter A. Starr, III (see note 4).

4.   Typescripts of letters from Starr to his family during 1926 27 were made available to the author by Walter A. Starr, III. The originals were handwritten for the most part, but Peter Starr's father evidently had them transcribed by a typist for use by the family. (The handwritten originals are in the possession of Ms. Eddy Ancinas, Peter Starr's niece.) A typescript copy of this particular letter, dated October 24, 1926, also appears at B. L. 71/293 C, CTN 2, Folder 25.

5.   Harold Boucher, Esq., telephone interview by author, 26 October 1998. Harold Boucher commenced work at Pillsbury, Madison & Sutro in 1934 and "inherited" Starr's secretary, who made the remark to Mr. Boucher. This remark was the only point of information about Starr remembered by Mr. Boucher. Otherwise, the law firm reported to the author that it had no information on Starr. See also *Starr's Guide*, ix.

6.   This photograph by Harley Stevens was used as the frontispiece for *Starr's Guide*. It was taken on a July 1932 expedition to climb Mt. Ritter.

7.   Clarence King was then 27 years old, and he went on to found the United States Geological Survey, becoming its first director. He wrote the classic *Mountaineering in the Sierra Nevada* (Boston: James R. Osgood and Co., 1872). For a day-by-day reconstruction of the 1864 expedition, see William H. Brewer with notes and introduction by William Alsup, *Such A Landscape!* (Yosemite N.P.: Yosemite Association, 1987).

8.   Leonard, *Mountain Records*, 69, 73.

9.   Starr Family Photo Album dated "1929–," made available to the author by Starr's niece, Ms. Eddy Ancinas; *Comments and Record*, 14 16.

10.   B. L. 71/293 c, CTN 10. See also *Comments and Record*, 19. The "Sierra Club" reference in the entry was an identifier stating the alpine organization, if any, with which the climber was affiliated. It did not mean that Starr was with a Sierra Club outing on that occasion (and, in fact, the 1930 High Trip had already passed by this peak four weeks earlier). Note also that at that time, the Sierra Club gave special recognition to its members who climbed all 14,000-footers in the Sierra.

11.   Quotations are from the introduction by Walter A. Starr, Jr., to the first edition of *Starr's Guide*.

12.   "The Mountain's Call" appears in full in Chapter 12 of this book and was originally published in the first edition of *Starr's Guide*. In a letter to Charlotte Mauk (undated) in 1961, Walter A. Starr, Sr., stated his approval of a short paper on his son by a student, and said Peter Starr "did considerable writing of poetry." B. L. 71/295 c, CTN 137, Folder 37.

13.   *SCB (June 1934)*, 81.

CHAPTER 2

14.   Glacier Lodge burned in 1999.

15.   *Sierra Club Bulletin* 1 (1894): 124.

16.   Steve Roper, *The Sierra High Route: Traversing Timberline Country*, 2d ed. (Seattle: The Mountaineers, 1997): 56 63.

17.   Walter A. Starr, *In Memoriam, Allen L. Chickering 1877 1958* (Sacramento: California State Library, c. 1958). A copy was provided to the author by the Starr family.

18. *Mountain Records*, 63.

19. *Climber's Guide*, 352.

20. Steve Roper, *The Sierra High Route: Traversing Timberline Country*, 2d ed. (Seattle: The Mountaineers, 1997): 62 63. Walter A. Starr, "From Yosemite to Kings River Canyon," *Sierra Club Bulletin* 20, no. 1 (1935). The latter article by Starr became controversial. Theodore Solomons increasingly felt, as his life progressed, that he had not been given sufficient credit for his pioneering explorations in search of what eventually became the John Muir Trail. When the 1935 article by Starr was published, Solomons took offense and felt slighted. Solomons complained that Starr and others were taking too much credit at his expense. See Shirley Sargent, *Solomons of the Sierra* (Yosemite N.P.: Flying Spur Press, 1989): 109 114.

21. Walter A. Starr, *My Adventures In the Klondike and Alaska* (San Francisco: Lawton Kennedy, 1960): iv-v.

22. Starr, *My Adventures In the Klondike*, iv-v.

23. Information from the author's interviews with Eddy Ancinas and Walter A. Starr, III, and Biographical Summary of Walter A. Starr, B. L. 71/103 C, CTN 35.

24. The original is in the possession of Ms. Eddy Ancinas. Copies were privately published later by Carmen Starr (see note 168).

25. Ranch Book for 1930–1940 in the possession of Ms. Eddy Ancinas.

26. *SCB (June 1934)*, 81; *NCSN*, 65.

27. *SCB (June 1934)*, 81.

28. The news articles are from a collection lent to the author by Glen Dawson; an overlapping collection is in the Norman Clyde Collection at B. L. 79/33 C, CTN 4, Seventh Folding File; see also *SCB (June 1934)*, 81–82.

29.   *SCB (June 1934)*, 81 82.

CHAPTER 3

30.   Mt. Davis, northwest of Banner Peak, is also in the Ritter Range but does not bear on the story.

31.   *Comments and Record*, 6.

32.   From Highway 395 near the Mammoth Lakes Airport, however, there is a viewing window into the region. From there, Michael Minaret can be seen as the thin needle just to the left of Clyde Minaret.

33.   Both Norman Clyde and Glen Dawson referred to the pass as Minaret Pass. See *Quest*; *Dawson-Farquhar 8/21/33 Letter*; and *SCB (June 1934)*, 83. The name has never been made official.

34.   John Muir, *The Mountains of California* (New York: The Century Co., 1894).

35.   "Journal of James T. Gardiner," July 12, 1866, quoted in Peter Browning, *Place Names of the Sierra Nevada* (Berkeley: Wilderness Press, 1986): 147.

36.   Ansel Hall and E. C. Solinsky, "Report of an Exploratory Expedition into the Mount Ritter Minarets Region September 8 to 20, 1922" (1922): 32. A copy is available in the Yosemite Research Library. For the 1924 reference, see note 40.

37.   Jim Snyder to Steve Medley, 17 February 1999 (on file at Yosemite Association, El Portal, California). In a subsequent letter, Mr. Snyder stated: "The ore discovered in the Minarets was marginal, but it seems few realized that in the heat of the moment and felt at the time that the inability of the district to produce more was due to the lack of transportation for the ore. Still, it was the claims in the Minarets that caused that part of Yosemite to be eliminated from the park in 1905. 58th Congress, 3d Session, Doc. No. 34, U.S. Senate, 'Report of the Yosemite Park Commission. Dec. 5, 1904,' 48 50, is a report on

the Minarets claims, noting that the district was organized in the summer of 1878. The miners claimed to have struck paying veins of silver, but they came to naught. In the twentieth century, the interest turned from precious metals to other metals including tungsten, even iron. Transportation remained a problem, and the sources continued to be marginal. There is a geologic study of the Minarets claims with histories of their development and potential in U.S. Geological Survey Bulletin 1516 A–D, King Huber, et al., *Mineral Resources of the Minarets Wilderness and Adjacent Areas, Madera and Mono Counties, California* (Washington: GPO, 1982). Huber's chapter discusses the geology while the chapter by Horace Thurber and others discusses the economic mineral appraisal of the Minarets Wilderness, claim by claim." Jim Snyder to author, 30 March 1999 (on file at Yosemite Association, El Portal, California).

38.　Most of the information in this paragraph is from two engineering reports: Hershey & White, *Consulting Engineers Report on Shadow Creek Venture* (July 11, 1929), and Hershey & White, *Preliminary Geological Report on The Fortune-Crown Point Group* (September 14, 1920). Copies of these reports are in the Yosemite Research Library. For consistency, Nydiver is spelled Nydiver herein although some references use Nidiver.

39.　See note 36.

CHAPTER 4

40.　C. W. Michael, "First Ascent of The Minarets," *Sierra Club Bulletin* 12 (1924): 28.

41.　*Yosemite Nature Notes* 46, no. 2 (1977): 25. Enid later became the first woman naturalist in the national park system.

42.　Steve Roper to author, e-mail, 20 September 1999.

43.　Steve Roper disagrees on the origin of "ducks." He says "duckstone" was an English boys' game wherein the object was to build a pile of rocks and knock off the top one with a stone hurled from distances of about twenty feet. The author suspects, nonetheless, that the usage perpetuated itself due to the duck-like silhouette that often results from piling two or three flattish rocks one on another, usually a small one on top.

44.   Michael left no summit note. He did pile a few stones together at the top. *Sierra Club Bulletin*, 12 (1924): 31.

45.   B. L. 71/293 C, CTN 10.

46.   Dennis Kruska, *Twenty-Five Letters from Norman Clyde, 1923 1964* (Los Angeles: Dawson's Book Shop, 1998).

47.   *Climbing*, 4.

48.   Norman Clyde, "Death on a Mountain Top," *Westways* (May 1934): 10. The three women were Dorothy Baird, Alice Carter, and Julie Mortimer. Clyde's *Westways* account of that excursion (on August 3, 1931) is gripping:

> The Sierra Club was encamped a few miles away and in it were a number of women climbers. As no woman had ever scaled these peaks, this group was anxious to make the first feminine ascent. I agreed to go with them. We made our first mistake when we started late. Thus, we did not reach the foot of the Minarets until about noon. After scaling a cliff we came to the margin of a steeply pitching and intricately crevassed glacier. Out came the ropes and we tied ourselves together. We crossed the glacier successfully but our progress was so slow that we did not reach the summit of the spire until about six o'clock.
>
> We halted only a few minutes and then started down. It was dusk when we arrived again at the glacier and unfortunately we couldn't find the steps in the ice that we had cut during our way up. Presently we were confronted with a crevasse of indeterminable depth. We turned aside, and there was another. There seemed to be no way out of our dilemma, and to make matters worse the sky was overcast, it was bitter cold, and we had no lights. There was only one thing to do, and that was to attempt to descend into the crevasses and to climb out on the other side.

After testing their depth with an ice-ax made fast to a rope and finding them comparatively shallow, I descended into the first on a rope attached to a belay in the ice. I reconnoitered the crevasse and found a feasible route out. It was as black as the inside of a checker in the cavern and little better outside. However, the entire party followed, including the women, none of whom had uttered a single complaint and all of whom had taken the entire grueling climb with fortitude and forbearance. We ascended the opposite wall of the crevasse, crossed the glacier and conquered the second crevasse in a like fashion and finally reached the foot of the mountain.

Presently the moon emerged from behind the clouds shedding a dim radiance over the jagged mountain looming menacingly above us. We ate the remnants of our lunch, uttering in the meanwhile silent prayers for our deliverance. But our troubles weren't over. The cliff we had ascended so readily earlier in the day must now be descended. There was moonlight, but it was of little assistance. Ultimately we found it necessary to descend by rope. We accomplished it safely, praise be, but to this day I don't understand how. Fifteen minutes later we had a roaring fire going in a group of pines growing on the margin of a lake. By then it was midnight and we were soon asleep, fatigued to the point of exhaustion.

49.   This description of Clyde is taken from a number of sources and combined into a single paragraph. Sources include Ted Waller, Glen Dawson, and the Lyhne-Eichorn interview.

50.   Clyde had a climbing companion on occasion. Julie Mortimer's name appears in many Sierra registers from the 1920s and 1930s, often with Norman Clyde's. *Climbing*, 3 4.

51.   B. L., Francis Farquhar Collection, c-b 517, ctn 2.

52.   *Comments and Record*, 15.

53.   *Mountain Records*, 90. Incidentally, Starr made the ascent on July 10, 1929. *Mountain Records*, 90.

54.   A copy of the note was provided to the author by Clyde scholar Mary Millman of Berkeley. Farquhar had known Clyde since at least 1914 when they climbed Unicorn Peak together in the Yosemite backcountry. *Mountain Records*, 36.

CHAPTER 5

55.   B. L., Oral History Transcript of Interview with Francis Farquhar, October 16, 1971. In addition, Farquhar's son, Peter Farquhar, provided the author with the following entries from his father's typed diary for August 1933:

> August 14—At lunch at BC, Vincent Butler and Walter Starr—great anxiety over failure of Pete Starr to return from Sierra trip—helped analyze the case; organized stand-by team of Sierra Club members. At Grabhorns' for dinner, word came that Pete's car and camp had been located; communicated with Glen Dawson and Jules Eichorn and set them on their way to lake Ediza and the Minarets; also sent out call for Norman Clyde.
>
> August 15—Felix Smith (Standard Oil attorney) brought Pilot Bush of SO Co. to my office, and in a short time I was at Presidio airport and took off in two-seater plane; flew over Yosemite, to Mount Ritter and around the Minarets; searched all streams and pools and snowfields, but no sign; "down draft' as we came close to wall of Minarets; landed at Bishop and spent the night there.
>
> August 16—Returned for another search of Minaret area, but still no sign; returned to San Francisco. Ground search continued. (Body ultimately found by Clyde) (See: SCB, 1934, 19:3, pp. 81 85; and, Starr's "Guide to the John Muir Trail.")

Years after his death, Farquhar remains the foremost historian of the Sierra Nevada. See *The History of the Sierra Nevada* (Berkeley: University of California Press, 1965); *Place Names of the Sierra Nevada* (San Francisco: Sierra Club, 1926); and William H. Brewer, *Up & Down California in 1860 1864* (New Haven: Yale University Press, 1930).

56.   See also the photographs of Farquhar in biplane in the Francis Farquhar Collection at Bancroft Library, some of which are reproduced in this book. The general route can be traced via Farquhar's aerial photographs. They flew over Yosemite Valley en route to the Minarets. They landed at Bishop in the Owens Valley, searched again on the 16th, then returned to San Francisco. Farquhar was not part of the ground search party.

57.   Original telegram made available to the author by Glen Dawson in 1998.

58.   In an e-mail letter to the author dated 13 October 1998, Glen Dawson described Richard Jones as follows:

> Richard Morse Jones was born October 10, 1912, the same year I was born. We grew up in the same neighborhood in Garvanza, a part of Los Angeles, and as boys, shared many experiences. Dick excelled in classes in tumbling and playing the harmonica, which I did not. We were members of a boys' organization named The Trailfinders. He went to Polytechnic High School where he was on the gym team. He worked for my father at Dawson's Book Shop in Los Angeles and spent most of his working experience at North American Aviation as an expediter. Dick was active with me in Ski Mountaineering and Rock Climbing sections of the Sierra Club and we made many excursions and climbs together, notably East Buttress of Mt. Whitney, and he led me up first ascent of Mechanics route at Tahquitz Rock. Dick's wife, Adrienne Jones, has written a number of books for young people.

Richard Jones died in 1997. Sierra Historian Bill Oliver of Los Angeles believes that Jones had no diary (based on interviews with Jones in 1990). Bill Oliver, telephone interview by author, 11 November 1998.

59.   The biographical information on Jules Eichorn is from the *Eichorn-Lyhne Interview* and Eichorn's oral history on file at the Bancroft Library. See also *Climbing*, 4. The comment about polemoniums is from Ted Waller, telephone interview by author, 8 June 1999.

60.   Glen Dawson, telephone interview by author, 9 October 1998.

61. B. L., 71/293 C, CTN 10.

62. *Eichorn-Lyhne Interview.*

63. B. L., 71/293 C, CTN 10. Walter Brem was also a member with Dawson of a boys' organization called "The Trailfinders." Glen Dawson to author, e-mail, 26 October 1998 (see note 58).

64. For the February 1932 issue of the *Sierra Club Bulletin*, Dawson authored "Mountaineering Notes: Mountain-Climbing on the 1931 Outing." In part, he wrote (at page 114):

> *The Minarets.* Jules Eichorn, Walter Brem and I went ahead of the main party to Garnet lake. We crossed a tiring 12,400-foot pass between Mount Lyell and Rodgers Peak. July 31st we left the lake above Garnet Lake to explore the Minarets and, if possible, find the highest. We had a copy of C. W. Michael's account (*SCB*, 1924, XII:I). We followed his route through the notch and up the chimney. The chock-stone which was his greatest difficulty we surmounted by *courte-echellei* to the "ladder with the lower rungs missing." We reached the top of Michael's Minaret two hours after we started in the chimney. While on top I was under the impression Mr. Michael did not climb the same peak. (There were several reasons, one of which was it is impossible to see Iceberg Lakes and Lake Ediza from the portal.) But we later decided that the peak we climbed is undoubtedly the same peak Mr. Michael made a first ascent of on September 6, 1923.
>
> Another hour's travel brought us to the Third Minaret—a first ascent. We followed the ridge still farther and climbed Clyde's Minaret, the peak above Iceberg Lakes to the left of the glacier. Homer D. Erwin (July 7, 1931) is the only person to climb the peak since the two 1929 parties (*Sierra Club Bulletin*, 1930, XV:I, page 190). We returned by way of Iceberg Lakes, keeping on the rocks and not going onto the glacier. We were out fourteen hours.

By using a hand level from the three major peaks of the Minarets we found that Clyde's Minaret is the highest, Michael's Minaret the second highest, and Third Minaret, which connects the other two, is third highest of the group. There is, however, very little difference in the height of these peaks. The left picture of Plate xiv in *SCB*, 1924, XII:I, is of Clyde's Minaret, taken from the portal below Michael's Minaret.

August 3d Norman Clyde took Julie Mortimer, Alice Carter, and Dorothy Baird up Clyde's Minaret. They came down the glacier after dark, experiencing some difficulty.

Michael had written that from The Portal he could see Iceberg Lake, Lake Ediza, and the Michaels' camp. *Sierra Club Bulletin* 12 (1924): 30. As Dawson pointed out in the quoted text, those landmarks are not visible from The Portal. By the time he wrote the article, Michael may have confused the scene with the vista from Michael's Notch.

65. In approximately 1990 in the *Eichorn-Lyhne Interview*, Eichorn said of this event:

> They couldn't make out for sure which was the higher one, whether it was Clyde's Minaret or Michael's Minaret. So when Dawson and I and a fellow by the name of Dick Jones decided to climb Michael Minaret and then traverse, which had never been done before, to Norman Clyde Minaret, we had with us a level and we could level from Michael Minaret towards Clyde's Minaret, and it appeared that Clyde's Minaret was just slightly higher. And so we came off of Michael Minaret and traversed to Clyde's Minaret, which is a long tedious climb because it was on a very, very sharp ridge with all sorts of pinnacles. You had to climb up and down, and up and down. The elevation actually, if you just sighted it, wasn't much but when you had to climb from one thing to another it was considerable. So we finally got to Clyde's Minaret in the afternoon and using our level, we sighted it back to Michael Minaret and found that Michael Minaret was not quite as high as Clyde's Minaret, and so we had established the fact that Norman Clyde's Minaret was the highest.

66. Eichorn later recalled:

> Thunderbolt Peak was named because I was the last man off of Thunderbolt Peak on its first ascent. The dog-gone thing was suddenly engulfed with a storm which was much further south of us, five minutes before the lightning and we thought it was perfectly OK for everybody to get off. Well, everybody got off all right. I almost didn't get off because when the bolt struck I was some 50, 75 feet away from the monolith which was Thunderbolt Peak. (*Eichorn-Lyhne Interview.*)

67. Glen Dawson to author, e-mail, 25 October 1998.

68. Bill Oliver, *The Sierra Echo* 36, no. 2 (March–April 1992). Eichorn recalled the same event in the *Eichorn-Lyhne Interview* as follows:

> We ended up . . . . Then we wanted to go down the west side and there was a storm brewing but it didn't seem particularly serious. But it ended up starting to rain and so we tucked ourselves under a huge boulder. I mean huge, maybe approximately 25, 30 feet in diameter which had been jammed in what we call a chute. It began to rain so hard that the water that had accumulated up near the top of the ridge was coming down and undermining underneath this huge boulder which forces out from underneath this thing, which was then becoming more and more dangerous because of more and more water coming down. If you can imagine enough water . . . cloudburst coming down as if it was a sudden waterfall beginning and pouring over you, and we were hanging on by your fingernails and with a toe hold that might have been an inch wide, and pressing yourself as close as you could to the rock. Fortunately, it was steep. If it hadn't been so steep we would have been killed, but being so steep and with our heads pressed against the rock, there was not very much possibility of something striking us on the head, although several rocks did strike me and one made about an eight-inch gash in my back. This water was raining down so much sand and gravel that it filled up my back pockets of my jeans, if you can imagine. And so, finally, after we've been exposed to that sort of cloudburst for about three-quarters of an hour, it lessened and we were able to climb down but we had left a

lot of our gear because we couldn't carry it with us from out underneath this great boulder and most of it was damaged. Our climbing rope had been tossed into the gully and many rocks and things had smashed on to it and we had some pieces of rope that were approximately, maybe nine feet long with horse tails on them, footer, so absolutely useless. So we had to abandon all that sort of thing and had to climb down individually and with wet rock, we were uncomfortable about some of the pitches. We were still approximately 300 feet from the base of the Devil's Crags, which doesn't seem like much but the Devil's Crags were built like a steep pitched roof house that comes down and then at the very last part where you have the vertical walls, you have about 300 feet of very, very steep wall, going all vertical fortunately, otherwise we wouldn't have been able to climb down at all. And of course there's always hand-holds and foot-holds and good climbers make use of every little crevice as you possibly can if you need to. So we were able to get down and there was a snow bank at the bottom, the edge of the Devil's Crags and this huge amount of water had cut through this snow bank with rock and water and made a path through the snow bank about six feet wide and the snow bank itself was approximately twelve feet high. And this was solid, summer snow and it just cut through like that if you had taken some sort of a bulldozer and made a wide path through it. It was remarkable. As it ended, we could not get back to the main Sierra Club camp in Middle Fork of the Kings because of the tremendous amount of water and the fact that we were at that late part of the afternoon where the sun went down. Why, the minute the sun went down we started to get cold and we had wet clothing. And somehow or another, somebody had some matches. We had in a waterproof case which was retrieved and we were able after a lot of effort to start a fire and make a campfire, in which we dried our clothes the best we could so we could sleep because we had no sleeping bags and just the clothes we had taken along on the trip, and which weren't that warm, particularly because we didn't think we were going to have any problems with the weather. It had started off as a very clear day. But we learned that you always have to expect something which you don't really believe is going to happen but sometimes does, and in this case was almost fatal to all of us.

69.   Ted Waller, telephone interview by author, 21 June 1999.

70.   The summaries in the text of the 1927 1933 High Trips are based on two historical essays by Bill Oliver in *The Sierra Echo* 33, no. 6 (November–December 1989) and *The Sierra Echo* 36, no. 2 (March–April 1992) of the Sierra Peaks Section of the Sierra Club, and Dawson, "Mountaineering Notes: Mountain Climbing on the 1931 Outing," *Sierra Club Bulletin* 17, no. 1 (February 1932).

CHAPTER 6

71.   Remaining with Chief Ranger Robinson for part of the time were Lowell Hardy and Whiting Welch, friends of Peter Starr, neither of whom qualified as mountaineers. Welch evidently joined the base camp at Ediza at some point inasmuch as Dawson stated afterwards that Welch was the one who identified a handkerchief strip found by Clyde as Starr's. Mike Sutro was the third friend. Sutro drove Starr's car back. *SCB (June 1934),* 81

72.   The 1934 *SCB* account was based in part on a letter written on August 21, 1933 by Glen Dawson to Francis Farquhar. Dawson provided a carbon copy of the full letter to the author. It contains substantially more information than was provided in the 1934 *Sierra Club Bulletin*. For consistency, this book quotes only from the original letter, insofar as Dawson's actions are concerned. The quotes differ slightly from the version printed in the 1934 *Sierra Club Bulletin*. Passages in the letter not reprinted in the *Sierra Club Bulletin* are reproduced in note 112.

73.   *SCB (June 1934),* 81 82.

74.   *Quest,* 65 66.

75.   Bob Tanner to the author, 11 March 1999. In the letter, the owner of Red's Meadow Resort stated:

> In the early 1960's, Arch Mahan told me that he went up Shadow Creek during the search for Walter Starr and he showed me where Starr had camped before climbing the Minarets. The location was before Lake

Ediza on the stream below Nydiver Creek at Shadow Creek just above a narrow, steep chute in the trail.

Although Arch never mentioned personally climbing the Minarets in search for Mr. Starr, he would have been involved in supplying search crews.

The cabin was removed by the National Forest Service in the 1960s, but was located just above Nydiver Creek on the north side of Shadow Creek, according to Bob Tanner, telephone interview by author, 18 March 1999.

76.   *Dawson-Farquhar 8/21/33 Letter*, 1; *SCB (June 1934)*, 82.

77.   Leonard Minaret was climbed on August 4, 1932 by Richard M. Leonard and Herbert B. Blanks. This was two days before Starr left the blood record on nearby Clyde Minaret. *Mountain Records*, 32. Ritter was first climbed by John Muir in 1872. Banner was climbed in 1883. *Mountain Records*, 22, 34.

78.   *Dawson-Farquhar 8/21/33 Letter*, 1.

79.   *Dawson-Farquhar 8/21/33 Letter*, 1.

80.   *Mountain Records*, 2. The 1932 Ritter ascent is based on Peter Starr's assorted photos, many with notes and dates in his own hand on the back, provided to the author by Walter Starr III, including a photo taken from the summit on July 4, 1932. The July 1932 photograph by Harley Stevens that served as the frontispiece for *Starr's Guide* was taken on this outing.

81.   The *Dawson-Farquhar 8/21/33 Letter* stated: "Mrs. Willard says she talked to Starr, Jr., on the evening of the 30th and told her that he was going to Kearsarge Pass." Mrs. Willard was Dorothy Willard, wife of the Mammoth Lakes photographer, Stephen H. Willard, who published fine-quality scenic postcards of the region. Bob Tanner, telephone interview by author, 18 March 1999. Mr. Tanner added that the Willards liked to camp at Lower Iceberg Lake. (There is one exquisite camp there, at the north end.) Ediza and Lower Iceberg are close, about

fifteen minutes apart on foot. Most likely, Mrs. Willard encountered Starr at either Ediza or Lower Iceberg.

CHAPTER 7

82.   *SCB (June 1934)*, 82.

83.   The editor's note in *Comments and Record* purported to quote the entry but garbled it in several ways, including the wrong date. Glen Dawson's letter to Francis Farquhar dated August 21, 1933, got the date correct. Inexplicably, the *Sierra Club Bulletin* account changed it to July 31.

84.   B. L., 71/293 C, CTN 13.

85.   The next entry was dated June 27, 1934. The Douglas Robinson, Jr., is not the same as (and has no relationship to) the Douglas Robinson, Jr., who wrote the introduction to the recent editions of the *Starr's Guide to the John Muir Trail and High Sierra Region.*

86.   *SCB (June 1934)*, 82; *Comments and Record*, 7 8.

87.   The author found the negatives from the last roll of film in Peter Starr's camera in a grocery-store box full of old materials in the basement of the Starr family ranch house near Mission Peak. With the permission of Walter A. Starr, III, the author printed the negatives, images of which are set forth on pages 72 and 76.

88.   *Mountain Records*, 69.

89.   *Mountain Records*, 7, 11.

90.   *SCB (June 1934)*, 82.

91.   B. L., 71-293 C, CTN 3.

92.   *Quest,* 66.

93.   *Quest,* 66 67.

94.   Clyde, Field Notebook, Aug. 16, 1933 (in possession of David Bohn and Mary Millman, Berkeley, California). These accounts, particularly the *Quest* excerpt, made clear that no ducks were discovered up to this point, an issue that seems confused in the condensed *SCB (June 1934)* summary (that part of which is not reproduced here).

95.   *Quest,* 67.

96.   *Quest,* 67.

97.   *Dawson-Farquhar 8/21/33 Letter,* 2.

98.   *Dawson-Farquhar 8/21/33 Letter,* 1 (handkerchief identified by Whiting Welch, Starr's fraternity brother and close friend as the type used by Starr). The *Sierra Club Bulletin* account said it "had been used to tie up a cut finger." *SCB (June 1934),* 82.

99.   *Dawson-Farquhar 8/21/33 Letter,* 1.

100.   *Dawson-Farquhar 8/21/33 Letter,* 1. The *Sierra Club Bulletin* account left out the brand of cigarette. Dawson's letter explicitly names the brand as Chesterfield. Starr's correspondence from his European trip in 1927 expressed a preference for Chesterfield cigarettes (see note 4). Later in life, Clyde misspoke when he remembered the brand as Camels. See *Climbing,* 5.

101.   *Dawson-Farquhar 8/31/33 Letter,* 1.

102.   *Dawson-Farquhar 8/31/33 Letter,* 1.

103.   *Dawson-Farquhar 8/31/33 Letter,* 1.

104. Meanwhile, there was talk at large that Starr might have drowned in the lake and the authorities began to consider possibly dragging the lake, although it was never done. *San Francisco Chronicle*, 13 August 1933, 13.

CHAPTER 8

105. *Quest*, 68.

106. *Dawson-Farquhar 8/31/33 Letter*, 2.

107. *Dawson-Farquhar 8/31/33 Letter*, 2.

108. *Dawson-Farquhar 8/31/33 Letter*, 2.

109. *Dawson-Farquhar 8/31/33 Letter*, 2.

110. *Quest*, 70.

111. Sierra Club Members Papers, Vincent K. Butler, Jr., B. L., 71/295 C, CTN 34. Butler's letter dated August 22, 1933, to his wife stated in part:

> Mr. Starr and Lowell Hardy spent most of yesterday with me and Jules Eichorn gave me a detailed report of their quest. The searching party did heroic work. . . . The conclusion seems inescapable that he fell, either during or after his climb to the top of the highest Minaret, and that he lies in the bergschrund or crevasse between the mountain rock and glacial edge. Mr. Michael [*Note*: The Charles Michael who had first climbed Michael Minaret in 1923, the assistant postmaster in Yosemite Valley], whom you may have met by this, will tell you what this means. It is highly improbable that his body would not have been found if it were discoverable. The mountaineers picked up the minutest traces, including small cigarette butts which were identified as Pete's.

112. *Dawson-Farquhar 8/31/33 Letter*, 2. For completeness of the historical record, the portion of the *Dawson-Farquhar 8/31/33 Letter* not printed in the June *Sierra Club Bulletin* was as follows:

Dear Francis: Since it was through you I went to look for Walter Starr Jr.
you may like some report of the search. Dick Jones and I left Los Angeles
a few hours after you telephoned from San Francisco. We arrived at the
Mammoth Ranger Station shortly after Jules and Mr. Starr (the morning of August 15). The same day we went into camp at Lake Ediza where
State Police, Forest Rangers, C.C.C. boys, and others had already taken
up the search. Norman Clyde and Oliver Kehrlein arrived late that night.
Starr Jr.'s camp was located across the stream [Shadow Creek] and a
few hundred feet above the cabin below Lake Ediza. [According to the
map drawn by Mr. Starr published in the *SCB* in 1938, Vol. XXIII (Plate
X), the trail was on the north side of Shadow Creek until shortly before
reaching Ediza, where it crossed to the south side.] It seems to me that
news of the camp being found should have started investigation by local
people, but it did not. Contrary to the opinion of others I believe the food
he had could have lasted him several days. The fact he left his crampons
and ice-axe and camera made other searchers believe he was not on high
mountains, but it only made me believe he was out to do real rock work.
Two C.C.C. boys climbed Ritter finding record of Starr Jr. dated July
30th. Mr. Starr says Starr Jr. left San Francisco on the 29th and Mrs. Willard says she talked to Starr Jr. on the evening of the 30th and told her
that he was going to Kearsarge Pass. Banner was climbed by Mr. Starr
and Dick [Allan] Starr, but no record was found of Starr Jr. ever having
climbed Banner. The morning of the 18th the five climbers searched the
east face of Banner without finding a trace.

This leaves the Minarets. Clyde and Kehrlein investigated the glacier on
Clyde or Highest Minaret (12,278) climbing the peak but did not find any
record on top. Whiting Welch, a friend of Starr Jr. and Mr. Starr were
both under the impression that Starr Jr. had climbed the Minarets before.
Clyde found a piece of handkerchief at Upper Iceberg Lake. The handkerchief was of a type used by Starr Jr. according to Welch. Clyde and
Kehrlein on the 17th followed a line of ducks up a daring route on Clyde
Minaret. The ducks ran out near the top. They were believed by Clyde
to be recent. One duck in particular had been placed on grass and the
grass was still green underneath.

❈   ❈   ❈

[Omitted portion appears in *SCB (June 1934)* with minor edits.]

❈   ❈   ❈

We saw you or that is the plane flying over the Minarets. This is getting quite long but I want to add that I am willing to help in any way in this or any other such matter. I am only sorry we could not get any more definite result. I believe solo climbing (except Clyde) should be discouraged, and hope that this great loss is the last one for a long time. May I thank you for asking me to go on such an important mission. I consider it a great honor.

Dick and I split the expenses which were $7.00 for 32 gallons of gas (we went 668 miles) and $4.00 for meals and lodging at Jerry K. for one full day and night.

Sincerely, Glen Dawson.

CHAPTER 9

113.   *Quest*, 70.

114.   Norman Clyde to Francis Farquhar, 4 September 1933. B. L., CB 517, CTN 1 (Correspondence A to C).

115.   The inventory list for the Norman Clyde Collection at the Bancroft Library includes a "Telegram H. C. Youngquist, giving information on Starr, rec'd 1:45 P.M. August 18, 1933." When the author asked for it, it turned out that the library could not find it. As explained in more detail in "A Comment on the Investigation," Mary Millman, fortunately, had saved a copy when she donated and catalogued the Clyde Collection.

116.   Clyde, for example, wrote in *Quest* (67) that "we paused and reconnoitered on the margin of Upper Iceberg Lake, lying on Minaret Pass a short distance northwest of Clyde Minaret at an elevation of some 10,000 feet." See also *Quest*, 72.

117. *Dawson-Farquhar 8/21/33 Letter*, 2.

118. Ted Waller, telephone interview by author, 19 March 1999. According to biographical information archived by the Sierra Club, Cliff Youngquist was born in 1887, was a civil engineer working for the Los Angeles Department of Water & Power, and was a member of the Los Angeles Chapter of the Sierra Club from 1932 1934. He was married, without children. B. L., 71/203 C, CTN 35.

119. *Quest*, 71.

120. *Climber's Guide*, 107, describes this U-shaped col as :

> *The Gap* (11,200+) is the wide, deep low point just southeast of Waller Minaret (Peak 11,711). Steep talus is found on the western side; slabs, cliff bands, and snowslopes are found on the Ediza side. Class 2; an ice axe is often needed.

It is referred to in the text of this book as the U-shaped notch to be consistent with Clyde and Dawson's contemporaneous writings.

121. *SCB (June 1934)*, 84.

122. Norman Clyde, Field Notebook for Aug. 19, 1933. Clyde was an advocate of carrying two types of boots—one pair with rubber soles for climbing on rock, and one pair with tricouni hobnails in the soles for climbing on snow or ice.

123. B. L., 71-293 C, CTN 9.

124. *Quest*, 71.

125. Three points deserve note concerning Clyde's footprint investigation. First, Dawson's letter to Farquhar said that on the 16th, the Eichorn-Dawson team returned to camp via the west side and then the broad U-Notch. Since this is north of Michael's Notch, they left footprints in the same region later scoured by Clyde for footprints. It would have been hard to distinguish those from any left by Starr, although Clyde found none anyway. Second, the threatened storms

that Clyde said had chased the climbers off the heights on the 16th and 17th would have eroded any footprints. Curiously, however, Clyde later said in an interview published in 1972 that "I knew there had been no storms." *Climbing*, 5. These conflicting statements are hard to reconcile unless the rain, though threatened, never materialized on the 16th and 17th. Third, and even harder to understand is how Clyde knew there had been no rain before Clyde even arrived on the 15th, rain that would have destroyed any footprints left by Starr. Later in the 1972 interview, in fact, Clyde said that "at the time the accident must have happened, little storms were going over the mountain," a comment Clyde used to suggest that perhaps Starr had been climbing on wet rock. How Clyde knew that is perplexing since he was miles away at the time. But, if it had been raining, as Clyde remembered in 1972, the rain would have dissolved any footprints in the area examined by Clyde. There is room to doubt the probative value of Clyde's footprint investigation.

126. Norman Clyde, Field Notebook for Aug. 22, 1933 (see note 94).

127. *SCB (June 1934)*, 84.

128. *SCB (June 1934)*, 84.

129. *Climber's Guide*, 107.

130. *SCB (June 1934)*, 84.

131. B. L., 71-293 C, CTN 19 (Unidentified Registers 1911 1920). While this scrap is filed under "unidentified registers" at the Bancroft, given its date, it is obvious that it is from Kehrlein Minaret.

132. *Quest*, 72.

CHAPTER 10

133. Introduction by Nicolas Clinch to Bancroft Library Oral History of Marjory Farquhar, (typescript, 1970). B. L., BANC MSS 200/96 C.

134.   *Dawson-Farquhar 8/21/33 Letter*, 2.

135.   The author found in the boxes in the basement of the Starr family ranch a large tattered envelope addressed to Walter Starr at the University Club in San Francisco from Ansel Adams, evidently returning wilderness photographs submitted by Starr. No comment or cover note was found.

136.   *Dawson-Farquhar 8/21/33 Letter*, 2.

137.   This chapter is based on two sources: Peter Farquhar, telephone interview by author, 25 March 1999; and Francis Farquhar's diary entry for August 24, 1933, provided by Peter Farquhar, which read as follows:

> Dinner party at 2728 Union Street; Ansel and Virginia Adams; Jules Eichorn; Marjory Bridge; Helen LeConte; Lewis Clark; Franklin Banker; Elsie Crail; Phil van Lubken; Emily Ambrose; Ethel Boulware; Mary Chamberlain; Helmut Leschke; Walter and Daisy Huber; Bourn and Anna Hayne; Bob and Ruth Lipman; Roger and Kay Simpson; Helen Simpson; Ralph and Pocas Reed; Helen Ashton; Miss Blood; Dorothy Bradner.

CHAPTER II

138.   *SCB (June 1934)*, 84.

139.   *Quest*, 73.

140.   *SCB (June 1934)*, 84 85.

141.   Clyde's was the last entry until Glen Dawson's brother, Muir Dawson, and two others made the ascent on August 9, 1936. *Mountain Records*, 31.

142.   *Quest*, 74.

143. *Climbing*, 5; Walter A. Starr, Sr., to Glen Dawson, undated, 2 (provided by Dawson to author).

144. For the record, Clyde's field notebook entry for August 25, the day he discovered Starr's body, reads as follows:

> Ascent of Michael Minaret; discovery of W. S. Clear, windless morning. Over meadows—flowers and up ridge—view of Iceberg Lake, an inky blue in morning shadows, morning light athwart the jagged minarets. Over talus and snow and up along ledge and up chimney to Michael's Notch; down in shadow—rock fringe—and along loose rock at base of minarets' view westward across basin containing several lakes to Merced group rather desolate; rugged one toward Ritter and Banner. Pass number of chimneys to southwest side of Michael Minaret; pause at bed of rock fringe; begin to climb broken face—details—eventually reach ledge and follow it to top of Michael's overhang; continue upward for some distance, attempt face but abandon it, go to notch—rather than difficult short pitch; gain notch [the Portal] and continue along ledge and up crest; traverse to right—details—directly upward again; reach crest and follow it eastward to summit about fifty yards sheer down to east and west. View of minarets, especially of highest—sheer face; sky filled with fluffy white cumulus clouds massed somewhat above Ritter and Banner.
>
> Remain for about twenty minutes after arriving at 10:45 and then return to notch; discovery from. Descend chimney and return by ledge and shoulder; through Michael's Notch and down past Iceberg Lake over meadows and through willows to Lake Adiza; on down trail to Agnew Meadow [a marginal note here says "bluebirds"]; from there by road to Mammoth.

Clyde's insert "—details—" suggested to the author the possibility that another portion of the field notebook had further details. Clyde historian Mary Millman, however, told the author that there were no further entries and that the word "details" was just Clyde's way to reinforce details in memory that he did not record.

CHAPTER 12

145.   May Albert, telephone interview by author, 22 December 1998. Albert was sixteen years old in 1933 and lived three blocks from the Starrs; she had been sent to Lake Tahoe to stay with friends while her mother stayed with Carmen.

146.   Walter A. Starr to Norman Clyde, telegram, 25 August 1933, 7:10 P.M. A copy of this telegram was provided by Mary Millman to the author.

147.   The reconstruction of the memorial service is from a letter written by Vincent Butler to his wife shortly thereafter. Sierra Club Member Papers, Vincent K. Butler, Jr. B. L., 71/295 c, CTN 34. The printed memorial brochure based on the eulogy contained a print of the last photograph from Ediza taken by Starr. The caption indicated that it had been taken "from his camp." This was a bit exaggerated, as the camp was actually ten minutes downstream, not at Ediza itself. Copies of the brochure are archived in Vincent Butler's Collection, in Norman Clyde's Collection, and elsewhere in the Bancroft Library. The Mallory description was taken by Butler from E. F. Norton, *The Fight for Everest* (London: Edward Arnold & Co., 1925): 145.

148.   Ted Waller, telephone interview by author, 19 March 1999. Waller recalled that Eichorn told him that Mr. Starr had "much discussion" with Eichorn over whether to try to remove the body.

149.   Clyde, Field Notebook, Aug. 27 28, 1933.

150.   *SCB (June 1934)*, 85. The others were Ranger Mace, Douglas Robinson, Jr., and Lilburn Norris (Norman Clyde, Field Notebook, Aug. 27 28, 1933).

151.   Norman Clyde, Field Notebook, Aug. 30, 1933.

152.   *Quest*, 74. The reference to Starr's Chute appears in the *Climber's Guide*, 117.

153.   Mr. Starr evidently stayed at the base and did not take the photographs from the Portal of Clyde and Eichorn climbing to Peter's ledge (see pages 116 and 117).

Those photographs were made with a camera other than the one normally used by Mr. Starr (which was the same camera, by the way, that had been used by Peter Starr). This is clear from comparison of the negatives. The negatives of Clyde and Eichorn taken from The Portal were smaller than the negatives made by the Starr camera. The author has examined them. The Starr camera negatives were large, measuring 2½ x 4¼ inches, whereas the Clyde/Eichorn negatives were smaller, measuring 2⅛ x 3¼ inches. There are no other negatives of the smaller format in all of the Starr family film reviewed by the author. This suggests the photos of Clyde and Eichorn were taken by someone other than Mr. Starr. Most likely, Mr. Starr stayed below with Ranger Mace (and took different photographs with his own camera). All of the extant negatives from this trip taken with the Starr family camera are, in fact, from the base of Michael Minaret (see page 114). Conclusion: the younger four climbed to The Portal and, from there, Clyde and Eichorn climbed to the body. This surmise is consistent with Clyde's statement that "four" climbed to The Portal and that Mr. Starr watched from "below" as he and Eichorn climbed to the body. *Quest*, 74.

154. Jules Eichorn to Glen Dawson, 11 September 1933 (made available to the author by Dawson).

155. Jules Eichorn to Glen Dawson, 11 September 1933.

156. In 1999, in response to the author's inquiry, Jules Eichorn indicated to his wife, Shirley Eichorn, that the body was placed in a canvas bag and moved to a crevice. Shirley Eichorn to author, 1 January 1999. His memory and health, however, were then failing. Other information provided by Jules at the same time was inconsistent with earlier, reliable recollections. The canvas bag point is, however, not inconsistent and is thus noted. It is also consistent with Clyde's recollection in 1972 in *Climbing*.

157. *Eichorn-Lyhne Interview.*

158. *Eichorn-Lyhne Interview.*

159. Claude Fiddler, telephone interview by author, 1999. Mr. Fiddler had gathered materials on Jules Eichorn a few years earlier, including this point.

160. *Climbing*, 6.

161. *SCB (June 1934)*, 85. Eichorn also stated, with respect to the slab, that he could "see still a place where this rock had been." *Eichorn-Lyhne Interview*.

162. Jules Eichorn to Glen Dawson, 11 September 1933, re-transcribed by Glen Dawson and made available to the author in October 1998.

163. Walter A. Starr, Sr., to Glen Dawson, undated; this handwritten letter was made available to the author by Dawson.

164. The group returned to camp above Lake Ediza and exited on the 31st. Clyde, Field Notebook, Aug. 31, 1933. It is noteworthy that in the same year (1933) on the opposite side of the globe, the ice-axe of George Mallory's climbing partner (lost when both men disappeared on Mount Everest in 1924) had been located in May. Mallory's body was discovered in 1999 by Conrad Anker, a Yosemite-based climber.

CHAPTER 13

165. Carmen's letter was inexplicably missing from the Norman Clyde Collection at the Bancroft. Photocopies were retained, fortunately, by Clyde Historian Mary Millman, who kindly provided copies to the author, as set forth in "A Comment on the Investigation."

166. Clyde's unfinished reply is at B. L., 79/33 C, CTN 4-5, Seventh Folding File, N-Z.

167. B. L., 79/33 C, CTN 4-5, Seventh Folding File, N-Z.

168. A copy can be found at the Bancroft Library under TYPZ239 2 G71 1960's.

169.   Redwell folder entitled "Score of Music Written By Walter A. Starr, Jr., 1914" (with contents) made available to the author by Walter A. Starr, III.

170.   This paragraph is based on several interviews by the author with Eddy Ancinas, Allan's daughter, between 1999 and 2001.

171.   B. L., 71-295 C, CTN 137, Folder 37; B. L., 71-103 C, CTN 35.

172.   A copy of the 1934 first edition is in the Bancroft Library (F868.S5S85).

173.   Vincent Butler died soon thereafter in a crash of a United Air Lines flight in the Rockies. Louis Butler, telephone interview by author, 10 February 1999 (Louis is Vincent's son).

174.   Glen Dawson to author, e-mail, 8 October 1998.

175.   See introduction to endnotes.

176.   Peter Browning, *Place Names of the Sierra Nevada*, 2d ed. (Berkeley: Wilderness Press, 1991): 208.

177.   David Brower, interview by author, San Francisco, 10 November 1998.

178.   Walter A. Starr, "From Yosemite To Kings River Canyon," a two-page typescript with a notation "Given to Richard M. Leonard 5/1/64—Written 'many years ago,'" provided to the author by Eddy Ancinas.

179.   For example, Ansel Adams, *An Autobiography* (Boston: Little, Brown & Co., 1985): 151.

180.   B. L., CB 517, Box 1.

181.   B. L., CB 517, CTN 1 (Correspondence A-C); see also *Climber's Guide*, 106.

182.   Walter A. Starr to Jules Eichorn, 11 December 1958 (date of postmark on

envelope); this handwritten letter was provided to the author by Shirley Eichorn in February, 2001.

183. Information on Walter A. Starr in this paragraph is based on David Brower, interview by author, San Francisco, 10 November 1998, and the family ranch book for certain years after Peter Starr's death.

184. Information on Allan Starr in this paragraph is based on interviews with two of his children, Ms. Eddy Ancinas and Walter A. Starr, III.

CHAPTER 14

185. Glen Dawson to author, e-mail, 23 November 1998.

186. Steve Roper, *Camp 4—Recollections of a Yosemite Rockclimber* (Seattle: The Mountaineers, 1994), Chapter 1.

187. *Climber's Guide*, 338. In 1999, Ted Waller told the author that he did not know this pinnacle had been named for him until about 1949 or 1950 on a Sierra Club High Trip when, camped beneath it, he consulted the *Climber's Guide* and saw that it bore his name. Waller recalled that in 1934 he and Eichorn had named it, half seriously, the "Wallcorn" Minaret. Ted Waller, telephone interview by author, 8 June 1999.

188. *Eichorn-Lyhne Interview.*

189. *Climber's Guide* in *Sierra Club Bulletin* 23 (1938): 32.

190. *Eichorn-Lyhne Interview.*

191. It is doubtful that Mr. Starr made it to The Portal, and it is likely that Eichorn carried the Starr camera to The Portal and made a series of photographs. From there, the tomb was visible, particularly with binoculars. It is not clear whether, in addition to viewing the gravesite from The Portal, Eichorn also climbed alone over to the gravesite from The Portal.

192.   Biographical information entitled "Jules M. Eichorn" supplied to author by Shirley Eichorn in booklet entitled "Mountaineering Pioneers—Profiles of Jules Eichorn, Dick Leonard, Dave Brower, Harvey Voge" by Robin Ingraham, Jr. (self-published, December 1998).

193.   In 1991, Jules Eichorn wrote the following notes about the meaning of music in his life:

> 2/13/91—I believe whatever beauty I express when playing the piano (or for that matter the clarinet, flute, French horn or trombone) came from my home environment, from the contact with Ansel Adams, Gertrude Field and the Sierra Nevada. Each contact made it possible for me to "hear" and "feel" what could be the most esthetically beautiful sound possible from beginning to end.
>
> All my family was musically inclined. My father and mother both sang and Dad particularly went further as he sang with the Deutche [sic] Maunerchor and other choral groups.
>
> Eleanor my sister still studied piano and as I remember had what was called then, "a lovely touch," and I am sure her playing influenced my interest in the piano.
>
> My contact with Ansel Adams was incalculable. It started with our family moving back to S.F. and getting in touch with neighbors who knew the senior Adams whose son Ansel heard me play and decided he would take me on as a pupil. This happened at age thirteen.
>
> 5/14/91—I did not know then how powerful a hold music had over me. However, I do know that I barely got through Lick-Wilmeding H.S. and had it not been for several very sympathetic teachers I would have certainly foundered in school. Since failing was not allowed a tutor was engaged and what with better study habits, etc., I was able to do my school work as well as practice the piano one to three hours a day.
>
> Ansel's approach to music was completely *different* from anyone else's. He had me play J. S. Bach and Beethoven in the main which developed my technique and gave me great music to listen to and express as well.

He also stressed mood, *tone*, *shading*, repose, thoughtfulness, rhythm, "breathing points," complete relaxation, contrast, inner shading, etc. In other words, ideas as to how beautiful musical quality could be attained. It was always how beautiful the music was and how it had to be expressed—As a result, in 1927 I entered the S.F. Piano Contest. I played a Scriabine prelude and won the second place prize at age fifteen. I naturally felt very good about this as there were over one hundred contestants and I was one of the youngest.

The next hurdle came after graduating from High School. The "great" depression was beginning and my father's business was failing and I had no idea what I would do except I strongly felt it should be in the area of music. My harmony teacher, Virginia Graham, was a lovely lady and had numerous connections in the bay area. [This was the last completed sentence in the extant materials.]

194. The outings are referenced in miscellaneous letters and information sheets provided to the author by Shirley Eichorn.

195. Glen Dawson, interview, Sierra Club Oral History Project (Bancroft Library): 6; Glen Dawson to author, e-mail, 25 October 1998.

196. *San Francisco Examiner*, 16 August 1934, a copy of which is in the Norman Clyde Collection at the Bancroft Library in CTN 4. By the author's observation, the gravesite is about halfway up from Thousand Island Lake to Catherine Lake, marked with an oval of stones embedded in the soil and a brass plaque bolted to a boulder stating:

> Here Rests
> Conrad-Anne
> Rettenbacher
> Who lost their lives
> Climbing Mt. Banner
> July 1934
> Die Naterfreunde Inc.
> San Francisco

197. Mary Millman, interview by author, Berkeley, 11 February 1999.

198. Aside from Clyde's own articles, Clyde's life is described in Smoke Blanchard, *Walking Up & Down in the World—Memories of a Mountain Rambler* (San Francisco: Sierra Club Books, 1985); Norman Clyde, *Close Ups of the High Sierra* (Bishop, CA: Spotted Dog Press 1997) that includes two excellent biographical sketches; Norman Clyde, *Norman Clyde of the Sierra Nevada: Rambles through the Range of Light* (San Francisco: Scrimshaw Press 1971); and Dennis Kruska, *Twenty-Five Letters From Norman Clyde 1923 1964* (Los Angeles: Dawson's Book Shop, 1998). A large collection of his papers resides at the Bancroft Library (B. L., 79/33 c).

CHAPTER 15

199. *Mountain Records*, 31.

200. The Clyde Minaret "register," like many in those days, was not a book but a series of paper and cardboard scraps with notations, usually stored in a discarded tin. In the case of the blood record referenced in the introduction of this book, the Starr entry is August 6, 1932. B. L., 71/293 c, CTN 5. A separate scrap from atop Clyde Minaret (71/293 C, CTN 10) has the following entry in bold letters:

W. A. Starr Aug 6 33

This scrap is a light-green, rectangular-shaped card measuring five by eight inches (approximately) with entries beginning 1929, including the Eichorn-Dawson-Brem entry from 1931. The purported Starr entry cannot be authentic. Clyde checked the register twice in August 1933 (once with Kehrlein) and found no such entry. It could not have been missed. Unlike the blood record that was loose on the summit, the card with the Eichorn-Dawson-Brem entry was never missing. Someone obviously added the Starr entry after the fact as a tribute to Peter Starr. (Nor could it have been Walter Starr, Sr., because he did not arrive in the area until August 14 and did not climb Clyde Minaret.)

At first, the author thought that one possible explanation was in the next entry by Richard Jones, Muir Dawson (Glen's younger brother) and others. They were on the summit on August 6, 1936, exactly three years after the date given in the fictitious entry. Perhaps, the author conjectures, they felt it was appropriate to make a gesture to Starr and dated it three years earlier to the day. In 1999, however, Muir Dawson reported to the author (via Glen Dawson) that his group did not do so. Glen Dawson to author, e-mail, 7 January 1999. It stated:

> I just talked to Muir on the phone. In 1936 he was just 15 years old. He is only surviving member of party that included Dick Jones, Bill Rice and Bob Brinton. It was a stormy day and they gave up the climb once and then went back late in the day to complete the climb. On top of Clyde Minaret it was raining and cold. A tarp had to be held over the register to keep it dry. He does not remember anyone signing Starr's name. They were so cold and wet he does not imagine any of the party thinking about anything but signing their own name and getting off the mountain. They did not get back to their camp until late at night.

201. *Comments and Record*, 13.

202. *Comments and Record*, 25.

203. *Starr's Guide* (11th ed.), x.

204. In one instance, the main text of *Comments and Record* quotes from "my diary." This confirms that Peter Starr kept a diary of field notes which he consulted back at home in completing his comments on routes intended for publication. A scorched-earth search of the Bancroft and many other sources by the author, including the attic of the former Starr home in Piedmont, failed to recover the diary itself or even the original guide manuscripts by Starr himself. The Starr family has concluded that they were probably thrown out when the family home in Piedmont was sold. See the chapter entitled "A Comment on the Investigation."

205. In 1999, Sierra historian Bill Oliver of Los Angeles confirmed this to the author. Bill Oliver to author, e-mail, 1 March 1999. Mr. Oliver saw the original register during his own ascent of Black Kaweah and sent the author a color photograph of the entry taken by Oliver on the summit (see page 141).

206. *Comments and Record* states in an editorial note:

> (Note: This was the first ascent of the east face of Clyde Minaret. The record left by Starr on the summit, as described, was found and recovered by Jules Eichorn in 1934 and was delivered to the committee on mountain records. It was found to have been marked on one end of the [original] record left by Norman Clyde in 1931—a piece of film carton box.)

When asked, Ted Waller no longer recalled this ascent, but did not doubt, based on the summit record, that he made it. Ted Waller, telephone interview by author, 8 June 1999.

207. *Quest*, 69.

208. *Quest*, 71.

209. Quoted in Chapter 9.

210. *Comments and Record*, 7 8.

211. Did Starr make an attempt on Clyde and turn back, constructing the fresh duck in doing so? It does not seem likely that Starr would try to duplicate his 1932 route (rather than a new one). Nor does it seem likely, if he had tried, that he would have failed in light of the excellent weather on August 1 and 2, 1933. The fresh-grass duck, relatively low in the chain of ducks, was likely made by the "unsuccessful" party referenced by Clyde. Too, the scouts would have seen Starr on August 2 had he been in the vicinity of the fresh duck.

212. B. L., 71/293 c, CTN 10.

213. In 1998, the author asked Glen Dawson if he knew anything about the entry by the eagle scouts and whether Clyde had ever made mention of it. Dawson said "If he did, I do not remember it." Glen Dawson to author, e-mail, 2 November 1998.

214. In an interview near the end of his long life, Norman Clyde made an oblique reference to the eagle scouts, stating "I knew that there had been no one in that area for several weeks before the accident except Boy Scouts. Since the climbing above there [the location of the fresh duck] was number four [Class 4], I didn't think they would go up there." *Climbing*, 3, 5. Clyde may not have remembered that the eagle scouts had, in fact, made the summit and that they had been on Clyde Minaret on August 2. The above oblique reference was the only time Clyde ever noted the eagle scouts, at least in any extant writing found by the author.

215. Based on his description of his usual camping gear in the introduction of the first edition to *Starr's Guide*, Starr did not have a tent, but probably had a tarp and sleeping bag.

216. B. L., 71-103 C, CTN 3.

217. The *San Francisco Examiner* reported on July 30, 1933 that Whiting Welch and Barbara Kruttschnitt were married in San Mateo in "one of the most brilliant society weddings of the season." See also *San Francisco Bulletin*, 29 July 1933.

218. United States Naval Observatory to author, e-mail, 31 December 1998.

219. Starr's crampons and ice-axe are now held by the History Department of the Oakland Museum.

220. *Comments and Record*, 28, 33.

221. Muir made the first ascent of Ritter in 1872 and painted a word picture of that view:

> Looking southward along the axis of the range, the eye is first caught by a row of exceedingly sharp and slender spires, which rise openly to a height of about a thousand feet, above a series of short, residual glaciers that lean back against their bases; their fantastic sculpture and unrelieved sharpness with which they spring out of the ice rendering them, peculiarly wild and striking. These are the Minarets. *The Mountains of California* (New York: The Century Co., 1894): 5.

222. It is fascinating that, coincidentally, on July 31, 1933, David Brower, the legendary climber and conservationist, was only a few miles to the north climbing Koip Peak and Parker Peak in the Yosemite backcountry. *Mountain Records*, 28.

223. As explained in "A Comment on the Investigation," the afterword in this book, Starr's original notes can no longer be found. The last known writing by Starr is his account of the Ritter ascent. It was copied verbatim into *Comments and Record* and thus survives in secondary form.

224. Starr did not cut his hands or fingers if Mr. Starr's letter to Glen Dawson, based on comments by Jules Eichorn, was correct that Starr's hands and fingers were "absolutely unscratched."

225. A bivouac at Upper Iceberg Lake would not have been in aid of going over Michael's Notch, for the direct route to that col is different, and, in fact, trying to get to Michael's Notch from Upper Iceberg Lake would have required substantial backtracking.

226. The *Climber's Guide* (117, 337) rates the "Amphitheater Chute" as Class 4. It was first climbed in 1958.

227. C. W. Michael, "First Ascent of the Minarets," *Sierra Club Bulletin* 12 (1924): 33.

228. *Sierra Club Bulletin* 23 (1938): 30.

229. On the descent, a climber can double the rope around a boulder or other secure hold and use the doubled rope for hand holds, pulling the whole rope down by one end after the pitch is completed.

230. *Climbing*, 5.

231. Eichorn once said: "He [Starr] should've been more . . . southeast on the base of [the final pinnacle of] Michael Minaret before he attempted to get to the summit, which was at that particular point only maybe two or three hundred feet

above him. But when he tried to climb the face of the thing, the northwest face, he pulled a rock and that was it." *Eichorn-Lyhne Interview.*

232. C. W. Michael, "First Ascent of the Minarets," *Sierra Club Bulletin,* 12 (1924): 31.

233. The *SCB (June 1934)* said the watch stopped at 4:30. Starr's niece, Eddy Starr, has possession of the watch. She let the author examine it. The watch has a tag attached to it by Walter A. Starr, stating: "This watch was carried by Walter A. Starr, Jr. (Pete) on his climb and fell with him from Michael Minaret. It was found on ledge below his body. W.A.S." By 1998, it was stationary at 4:23.

CHAPTER 16

234. Steve Roper to author, e-mail, 20 September 1999. Paragraph breaks were inserted by the editors.

MISSING IN THE MINARETS

This book is set in Fournier, an elegant typeface
originally designed by Pierre Simon Fournier before 1742 and
cut for hot metal composition by Monotype in 1924.

Designed by Sandy Bell
Springdale, Utah

Map on page 30 by David Fuller, DLF Group

CPSIA information can be obtained
at www.ICGtesting.com
Printed in the USA
LVHW030837290819
629174LV00003B/3/P